Living by Grace

BOOKS BY WILLIAM HORDERN
Published by The Westminster Press

Living by Grace

New Directions in Theology Today:
    Volume I—Introduction

The Case
    for a New Reformation Theology

Living by Grace

by
WILLIAM HORDERN

THE WESTMINSTER PRESS

Philadelphia

Scripture quotations from the Revised Standard
Version of the Bible are copyright, 1946 and 1952,
by the Division of Christian Education of the
National Council of Churches, and are used by
permission.

Book Design by Dorothy Alden Smith

Published by The Westminster Press®
Philadelphia, Pennsylvania

PRINTED IN THE UNITED STATES OF AMERICA

In Memory of Bob
We were brothers by birth
and friends by our free choice

Library of Congress Cataloging in Publication Data

Hordern, William.
   Living by grace.

   Includes bibliographical references and index.
   1. Justification. I. Title.
BT764.2.H66   234′.7   75-6548
ISBN 0-664-24763-6

CONTENTS

PREFACE

THIS WORK is an essay in practical theology. All too often in North American seminaries the term "practical theology" has the connotation of "how to do it" training. Practical theology is the discipline that teaches us how to preach, teach, and counsel. But in a deeper sense practical theology is the discipline of looking at the practice of the church in the light of its theology. In this work I attempt to view critically the common practices of Protestant churches in the light of the claim of Protestantism to be based upon justification by grace alone through faith alone. I advance the thesis that our practice all too often refutes our theological theory. Systematic theology is never complete until it has become practical theology. No theological theory can be complete without asking what it means for practical life and action.

I wish to express a word of gratitude to three persons who read this book in manuscript form and helped me to make important improvements. First, there is my wife, Marjorie. As always, her practical mind and critical eye have helped me to keep this study closer to life. Thanks also go to my colleague, Roger Nostbakken. His theological scholarship and knowledge of Luther's thought made him a valuable critic. My son, Richard, also gave this work a careful reading and made many helpful suggestions in the light of his M.Div. thesis on Law and Gospel. Needless to say, I make no attempt to blame these readers for the weaknesses that remain.

A special word of thanks to my secretary, Sandra Soderstrom, who worked through my mangled first draft and produced a beautifully typed copy.

W. H.

Lutheran Theological Seminary
Saskatoon, Canada

I

Introduction

THE DOCTRINE of justification by grace alone through faith alone was at the center of Protestantism from its beginning. The beginning of the Reformation is often dated from the time when Luther caught the significance of the Biblical statement, "The righteous shall live by his faith" (Hab. 2:4; quoted in Rom. 1:17; etc.). Later, in the Smalcald Articles, Martin Luther summed up the importance of the doctrine by saying, "On this article rests all that we teach and practice against the pope, the devil, and the world." [1] In a similar vein, John Calvin described justification as "the principal hinge by which religion is supported." [2] In the name of this doctrine, Luther and Calvin threw their thunderbolts at the "works-righteousness" of the medieval church. As the major Protestant churches developed, almost all of them made justification a cornerstone of their systems of doctrine. Yet today we must ask whether Protestants really understand, or believe in, justification.

Protestantism's Lost Doctrine

If Protestants do understand and believe their central doctrine, they obviously have not managed to communicate this to the world outside the church. As one discusses religion with unbelievers, a major argument that they use is as follows: "The Christian cannot be truly good, because he acts to win a reward or to escape a punishment. The atheist can be truly good, because he does the good for pure love of it and not for any hope of reward." When one tries to answer such skeptics by saying that the whole point of justification by grace alone through faith alone is that Christians do not do the good for the sake of any reward, the skeptic usually is unpersuaded because his observation of the believers in action does not fit this interpretation.

Furthermore, as we discuss the faith with the believers themselves, it often becomes evident that they define the Christian in terms of one who does certain things or, worse still, in terms of one who does not do certain things. In fact, being Christian is often equated with being a generally decent neighbor, a good citizen, and a reliable parent.

No denomination has done more than the Lutherans to emphasize the doctrine of justification. Justification has held a central place in Lutheran confirmation teaching, is written firmly into the confessional and constitutional statements of Lutheran churches, and it is probably the most frequent of all themes heard from Lutheran pulpits. And yet two recent studies of Lutheran opinions reveal a serious lack of understanding of this doctrine. A 1970 study of Lutherans in the Detroit area found that a majority of the laity believed that they could achieve salvation by keeping the Ten Commandments.[3] In 1972 there appeared a major study based upon an in-depth questionnaire given to 4,745 representative Lutherans between the ages of fifteen and sixty-five. This study found that about 40 percent of Lutherans are what the authors call "law-orientated" and given over to a legalistic way of life quite out of keeping with Lutheran theology.[4] This study also found considerable tendencies toward a works-righteousness in the remaining number of Lutherans. For example, 59 percent of the total agreed and only 34 percent disagreed with the statement, "The main emphasis of the gospel is on God's rules for right living." [5] Both of these studies found a radical difference between the opinions of clergy and laity. The authors of *A Study of Generations* found that "belief in salvation by works is resoundingly rejected by pastors but not by laymen." [6] Obviously Lutheran pastors have failed in communicating this doctrine to the laity. Quite probably, studies of other Protestant denominations would find similar patterns.

A study of attitudes of North American members of several denominations did find that 89.6 percent of the clergy and 69.2 percent of the laity reacted positively to the statement, "The more I support the church financially, the closer I feel to it and to God." [7] This indicates that most clergy and laity put such a high priority on giving to the church that it has become a work to perform in order to bring them closer to God. At the time of the Reformation this belief was abroad but condemned by the Reformers as works righteousness. Interestingly enough, the same study found that 45.5 percent of the respondents placed "gratitude to God" as the most important reason for giving. This, of course, is in keeping with Protestantism's emphasis upon justification. But the two answers together indicate confusion in the minds of church members. Is giving an act that we do in order to get closer to God or is it something that we do because God has got close to us?

One of the persistent questions raised by human beings is, Why did this happen to me? Behind the question lies the belief that it ought to pay to be good. If there is a God, surely he will see to it that people receive their just deserts. When, therefore, people are struck with tragedy, misfortune, or defeat, it is natural for them to ask what sins could have brought about this state of affairs. Since unfortunate persons can usually find someone who is obviously no more righteous than they who does not suffer the same ills, the cry goes up to heaven, Why to me? It would seem, however, that people who have been reared in the doctrine of justification would see things differently. They would be able to understand why Jesus said that it is a mark of God's love that his sun shines on good and evil alike and his rain falls alike on just and unjust (Matt. 5:45). The doctrine of justification teaches that the Christian's relationship to God is not based upon merit and thus service to God is performed out of love and not for the sake of any reward. Therefore, believers in justification should not expect that a life of goodness would preserve them from the misfortunes that afflict the less righteous. But, in fact, as one counsels with Protestants struck by misfortune, there appears little evidence that they are any less prone than others to demand that God reward their good deeds with protection from calamities.

Reinhold Niebuhr, analyzing the ironies of the history of the United States, found that the Calvinistic and Jeffersonian heritages combined to give the view that "providence intervenes to punish vice and to reward virtue." [8] Instead of seeing the sun shining on good and evil alike, people were stimulated to make every natural favor or catastrophe meaningful in moral terms. This led to particular dangers, Niebuhr said, in a nation where the natural wealth made it inevitable that there would be "more signs of favor than of judgment." [9] Throughout its history America has remained particularly susceptible to religious teachings which promise that being good or Christian will result in happiness, wealth, health, and all desirable things. Inasmuch as the United States has been predominantly influenced by Protestantism throughout its history, we have to conclude that this view of

Providence neatly rewarding good and evil is further evidence of the failure of Protestants to communicate effectively their doctrine of justification. The doctrine of justification centers in the affirmation that God graciously forgives our sins. We do not have to make ourselves worthy before we can come into his presence. Rather, he accepts us as we are. We are not condemned to a vigorous attempt to prove that we are good. Therefore, one would assume that Protestants, on the whole, would not be troubled with unresolved feelings of guilt, which modern psychology has found to be one of the persistent threats to mental health. It is difficult to get exact information on such a question, but as one talks with Protestant clergy he finds little evidence that, in their counseling of their parishioners, they find fewer problems of guilt than would be found elsewhere. Speaking personally, the bulk of my counseling in recent years has been with Protestant seminary students. I have been dismayed to see that problems of guilt are widespread in this group. I have been even more dismayed to find that all too frequently seminary students have not found that the doctrine of justification is able to speak to their problem. It seems reasonable to assume that when a person comes to seminary this marks him or her as being somewhat more literate in the faith than the average church member. If this is so, then the failure of this group to find in the doctrine of justification an answer to their problems of guilt is evidence that Protestants as a whole have failed to see how the doctrine of justification speaks to such problems.

Practice Speaks More Loudly than Words

Various reasons may be advanced for the failure of Protestant churches to persuade their constituencies about

justification. For example, it might be argued that original
sin being what it is, people naturally look to works-righteousness despite the teaching or preaching of their church.
No doubt there is some truth in this. However, my
observation of the churches in action leads me to believe
that a major aspect of the problem is that Protestant
churches *practice* a works-righteousness that speaks more
loudly than the words with which they teach justification.

This practice of works-righteousness begins with our
efforts to "sell" religion. A few years ago I heard a Roman
Catholic priest say that the great heresy of North American
religion is that we tell people that they ought to be religious
because "it is good for them." This describes many of the
efforts made to win people to religious commitment in our
culture. And, of course, this means that works-righteousness is involved at the very beginning of our religious life.
The basis of works-righteousness is the concern to do
certain things in order to win a reward or to escape a
punishment. In short, its fundamental motivation is that "it
is good for you."

A traditional form of evangelism threatened eternal
punishment in hell while offering the promise of eternal
bliss in heaven. Caught thus between the stick from behind
and the carrot in front, the candidate for conversion rather
plainly got the idea that, for his own good, he had better get
on the bandwagon and do the appropriate things to assure
his heavenly reward and escape the gates of hell. In the
"now" spirit of our North American culture, the fear or
hope that is delayed until after death loses much of its
motivational power. And so, while in some quarters evangelism still makes much of heaven and hell, even in these
quarters there is a growing tendency to spread Christianity
by emphasizing its rewards in this life. Emphasis is put
upon the unhappiness, the emptiness, and the estrangement

of those who do not have Christian faith. Over against this we are told of the happy, healthy, well-adjusted Christians. A few years ago a typical sign was put in New York subways which read, "Go to church next Sunday and leave your cares." In an even crasser vein we are regaled with stories of businessmen who win economic success through prayer.

During 1973, Christian churches banded together into "Key 73," which was one of the most thoroughly ecumenical attempts ever made to spread the gospel to all North Americans. To launch this campaign there was a television program. The message intended by the program was not too clear. However, we were shown a series of happy, well-adjusted middle-class Christians, and the message seemed to be that if the viewer would embrace Christianity, he too could be happy, well adjusted, and middle class. When Jesus wanted disciples he called upon anyone who was willing to take up his cross to follow him. Key 73 did not have much to say about taking up crosses. But Key 73 was neither better nor worse than Protestantism in general has been. Our primary method of evangelism for a long time has been to persuade people how good it will be for them if they become Christian. We have said little about the cost of discipleship.

Toward the close of the Key 73 year there appeared in *The Christian Century* a letter by a Jewish rabbi, Myer S. Kripke, written to a "kind lady" who had written to him, in the spirit of Key 73, to ask that he accept Christianity. It includes this very perceptive passage: "In your letter you speak again and again of finding peace in the joy of forgiveness. Will you understand me if I say that I find this quest for peace selfish and immoral? In a world where Americans have dropped bombs in Indochina daily; where Arab terrorists roam about and are encouraged by United Nations resolutions to kill innocent people at random, where millions of people are regularly insulted and exploited and more millions are kept hungry and shelterless—in such a world can you be satisfied with the 'peace' you find in the sense of forgiveness? Can you speak morally of finding peace—for yourself?" [10] The irony of this letter is that the rabbi obviously has a much deeper understanding of the spirit of justification than does the lady who is trying to convert him. As we shall see in a later chapter, Luther found the mark of the justified person in the loss of concern for a personal salvation and a willingness to be damned if that be God's will. It may be ironical that the Jewish rabbi has more of this spirit than his would-be converter, but it is not surprising. After all, Jesus' teaching was firmly rooted in the Old Testament. On the other hand, we cannot be too harsh on the anonymous "kind lady," because so much of the church's evangelism in recent years has been directed at the self-interest of the potential convert.

The problem with such evangelism is that once we have persuaded someone that he should become Christian because it is good for him, we have firmly implanted in him the idea that there is something that he had better do in order to escape the threats and win the rewards. In such a situation, if we tell him that he is to be justified by grace through faith, he will almost inevitably see faith in terms of believing the teachings of the church. This leads to what Bonhoeffer called "cheap grace." In the medieval form of works-righteousness, people were called to perform rather costly and sacrificial works to earn their salvation. But it seems that Protestantism has substituted a pretty cheap work to perform—just believe the proper doctrines and all will be well with you. In a later chapter I shall attempt to show why it is important to see that justification through faith is by no means justification through belief.

Works-righteousness is rooted in the idea that certain

actions must be performed to escape punishment and to win
reward. Normally this takes the form of a legalistic system
of rules and regulations that must be obeyed in order to
achieve the desired goals. Once again we find that, in
practice, Protestant churches are spreading a works-righteousness even while preaching justification. A few years ago
Langdon Gilkey noted that if the average church member is
asked what distinctive conduct is implied by church membership, about the only answer we would receive is "Giving
of my time, energy, and substance to the activities of the
church." Gilkey calls this "an excellent medieval 'works'
answer." [11] The laity have come to this point because, by
and large, their churches have put more emphasis upon such
activities than upon anything else. People are continually
exhorted to give more of their time, energy, and substance
to the activities of the church and those who do not respond
are usually made to feel that they are somewhere in the
outer darkness.

When a congregation distinguishes its "active" from its
"inactive" members, almost invariably the distinction is
based solely upon attendance at worship services and the
giving of money. One prominent American denomination
has even written into its constitution for congregations the
following definition: "Confirmed members who have received Holy Communion or made a contribution of record
to the congregation within the preceding year shall be on
the active roll of such members. . . . Those confirmed
members who no longer qualify for that roll because they
have neither received Holy Communion nor made a contribution of record to the congregation within the preceding
year shall be classified as inactive. . . . An inactive member
shall be restored by the church council to the active roll of
confirmed members when he again receives the Lord's
Supper and makes a contribution to the congregation." The

congregations are encouraged by this document to limit the
eligibility to vote to the active membership. Members are
thus informed that they pay for active membership either
by attending one Communion service or by giving one
recorded donation to the congregation. When they have
fallen from grace into inactive membership they have to
earn their way back by paying the price of both communing
and giving. Only then will they be restored to active
membership with all its rights.

If pressed, most Protestant churches would affirm that
they do not equate being an active member and being in a
saving relationship to God. The prerequisites for voting in
congregational matters are not necessarily the same as those
for admission to the Kingdom of God. But the average
person is likely to find such distinctions a bit too subtle to be
convincing. The practice of the church in defining active
membership tells the members rather clearly that the way
for them to get on the salvation bandwagon is to buy a
ticket by attending worship services and giving regularly.

Earlier we saw that Protestants express the works-right-
eous view that giving to their church brings them closer to
God. This attitude has certainly been encouraged by the
view that giving keeps a person in active membership. It
has also been encouraged by much of the "stewardship"
literature used by Protestant denominations. For example,
on the offering envelope supplied by my church, I recently
read this appeal: "You can't take your money with you. But
you can send it on ahead. You can build up financial
reserves in heaven, where it will yield satisfying dividends
through eternity." It would be difficult to find a more
eloquent expression of works-righteousness in the writings
of the medieval churchmen against whom Luther and
Calvin launched the Reformation.

Another area of practice by which churches spread the

idea of works-righteousness appears when they operate institutions such as colleges or schools. What distinguishes a "Christian" school from a secular one? All too often the distinguishing marks are compulsory attendance at chapel and/or a set of stricter regulations governing intersexual relationships, drinking, and, depending upon the denomination involved, perhaps dancing, smoking, or card playing.

Compulsory attendance at a chapel service is, in itself, contradictory. Presumably the purpose of chapel is to worship God, but the essence of worship requires that it be freely given. Worship that is enforced is no longer worship. Looked at from the point of view of justification, compulsory chapel attendance speaks very loudly. Students, in chapel because they do not want to suffer the punishment for not being there, may hear a sermon proclaiming that justification is through faith alone. But which will be more persuasive—the words of the preacher eloquently proclaiming that we are not saved by our works, or the practice of the institution, which demonstrates its Christian nature by forcing the students to perform the good work of attending chapel? Does not the practice loudly proclaim that Christians are people who perform certain acts? So important are those acts to being Christian that a Christian institution must force those who do not do them willingly to do them under penalty of chastisement. One can be thankful that, in recent years, the requirement of compulsory chapel attendance seems to be disappearing from church schools. But the memory lives on and church institutions usually have other practices that teach the same thing.

When a Christian college is distinguished from a secular one by stricter rules and regulations to govern the social lives of students, this practice teaches that Christians are people who live by a set of rules. Usually the institution

says that it enforces such rules because a Christian institution has to offer a witness to the world. We may agree with
the goal, but what is the nature of the witness given by such
rules? Is it not a witness to the idea that the performance of
certain things or, more obviously, the not doing of certain
things, is what decides whether or not one is Christian?

Whether in a congregation or in a church institution, all
too often the impression is given that only the respectable
and well-behaved are welcome. In the city where I live, a
Christian institution that was organized to give meals to the
needy refuses to serve persons with liquor on their breath.
This is but one of many ways in which the church and its
institutions tell people that first they must measure up to the
reigning views of propriety and respectability before they
will be welcome. The message comes through pretty
clearly; you earn your way into the church (and thus into
God's good graces) by learning to shape up.

Jesus scandalized the religious leaders of his time by
being a friend of the sinners and the outcast. But the
church that bears his name has seldom won recognition as a
haven for these groups. Churches are not as crude as those
secret societies that blackball undesirable candidates for
membership. But they have their own effective ways of
letting the undesirables know that they are not wanted in
the fellowship of the "believers."

Another practice of the churches that speaks against
justification is the prevalent tendency to set up a special
standard of conduct for the clergy. Of course, this is a
serious violation of another Protestant doctrine—the priesthood of all believers—but here we are interested in how it
witnesses against justification. Some actions that are legitimate (more or less) for the laity must not be performed by
the clergy—at least not in public. The specifics for the
clergy's conduct may vary from denomination to denomina-

tion, and, even within the same denomination, may vary
from one geographical region to another. In some cases
candidates for ordination must take an oath that they will
not smoke; in other cases they must pledge themselves to
total abstinence from liquor. Some of the clergy are not
allowed to play cards, dance, engage in any form of
gambling, go to X-rated movies, and so on. More universally it is forbidden to the clergy to swear, tell dirty jokes, or
laugh when others tell them. Until recently divorce was an
unforgivable sin for the clergy in almost all Protestant
denominations. If this has changed somewhat in recent
years, it is because of a more liberal view toward divorce in
general rather than an easing of the view that different
conduct is required of the minister. Whatever form it takes,
Protestant churches seldom require the same standard of
conduct for the laity that is required for the ordained
clergy.

Of course, Protestant denominations admit that the
clergy, like all believers, are sinners. Complete perfection is
not demanded of them, and some of their sins will be
forgiven with relative ease. It is, however, significant to see
what are the forgivable and unforgivable sins. It is not often
that one of the clergy is defrocked for racial discrimination,
for supporting unjust wars or for holding economic and
political views that support the rich and powerful at the
expense of the poor and oppressed. But a member of the
clergy quickly finds that indiscretions in the area of sex or
personal finances are unforgivable. Homosexual tendencies
almost universally will keep a person from being ordained.
Ministers can be compulsive eaters and suffer no more than
a few jokes about their waistlines, but if they become
alcoholics they had better be prepared to turn in their
clerical collars. We have mentioned that the clergy is
forbidden to gamble, but there is one exception. If the

gambling is done on the stock market, it is more likely to win respect than to cause offense.

This double standard of ethics that divides clergy and laity is sometimes spelled out in the constitution or laws of the church, but more frequently it is an unwritten set of laws. They are sanctioned by the general acceptance of the clergy, the firm supervision of the denominational hierarchy, and the fervent demand of the laity.

Apart from the implications for the priesthood of all believers, what does this practice of the double standard teach? It tells people that the leaders of the church are expected to set an example of higher rectitude. Inasmuch as the church requires these higher standards from its leadership, this implies strongly that the primary purpose of the church is to develop in people certain standards of conduct.

But the nature of the higher conduct demanded of the clergy is very significant. As we noted, it does not call the clergy to be outstanding in terms of social conscience, love for neighbor, or even in being forgiving. The rules applied to the clergy are primarily matters of personal conduct and have to do with the development of a personal piety and purity. As we shall see in a later chapter, when a religion embraces works-righteousness, these are always the kind of works that it extols as the way to salvation. The whole practice of the double standard for clergy and laity is thus a concrete way of teaching works-righteousness.

Finally, we might note that ordained ministers are usually dismissed with dispatch when they break the more serious of these rules. This plainly says to people that, when the chips are down, the church does not live by forgiveness. If the clergy have to justify themselves by works, how credible can they be when they teach that justification is by grace alone through faith alone?

If we are correct in finding that the practice of Protestant churches has contradicted the teaching of justification, does this indicate that there is some serious weakness in the doctrine itself? Is it, in fact, unlivable? After all, can we really expect that people will become Christian if we do not persuade them that Christianity is good for them? We may hope that, having been won to the faith, they will be opened up to more selfless conduct, but must we not start by appealing to them where they are? And where they are is surely centered in a concern for the self. Can we expect to win a self-centered person to Christianity if we cannot persuasively answer the question, What's in it for me?

Furthermore, if the church is to proclaim the gospel, it must have an organization and that organization must be supported. So, is it not imperative that attendance at church services, financial support of the church, and general support for its programs be emphasized? If a person can be a member in good standing in a congregation where he is never seen except at baptisms, funerals, or weddings, does not the whole business of the church become a farce? Even if such good works as church attendance and support do not earn salvation, can any church survive that does not emphasize such activities? Given the sloth of human nature, is it not necessary to provide stimulus to such activities by exhortation and by dropping the nonactive from full rights of membership or even from membership itself?

Finally, is it not an imperative task of the church to witness to righteousness? If flagrant sinners are welcome in church circles, will it not undermine the moral standards of the community? If church-supported institutions do not enforce higher standards of conduct than secular ones, what do they have to contribute? In an age of ethical and moral decay, such as ours, is it not necessary for the church to set

forth standards of higher morality? Even the secular world
expects this. Tax concessions are given to the churches by
and large because churches are expected to uphold the
moral standards necessary to decent life in society. Would
it not be tragic if the churches fell below the expectations of
the secular world? And, that being the case, is it not
essential that the church be led by a clergy that sets an
example of a higher form of righteous living?

These are serious questions and always such questions are
raised when the church is criticized for practice that leads
to a belief in works-righteousness. But where then is the
doctrine of justification by grace alone through faith alone?
It is the purpose of this study to attempt to analyze the
meaning of Protestantism's central doctrine in a way that
will both help to clarify its meaning and show how it relates
to the objections just noted.

Justification Based Upon Jesus Christ

Justification is normally thought of as a Pauline doctrine.
Certainly it is Paul who used the term most frequently.
When the Reformers used Biblical references to prove the
doctrine, they usually quoted from Paul. Jesus did not use
the phrase "justification by grace alone through faith
alone," and some have even argued that the doctrine was a
perversion of Jesus' teachings by Paul and the early church.
However, it will be my thesis that, while Paul popularized
the phraseology of justification, the essence of the doctrine
is at the center of Jesus' life and teaching as portrayed in the
four Gospels. Therefore, I shall draw far more heavily upon
the Gospels than upon the Pauline teaching. This is done,
not to disparage Paul, but to emphasize that the doctrine is
rooted in Jesus and his mission.

Next to the life and teachings of Jesus, the most important

source upon which I shall draw is the writings of the Reformers. Luther and Calvin are generally extolled as heroes of the faith in Protestant circles. Generous compliments are paid to them, particularly around the time of the anniversary of the Reformation. Yet I find that Protestants fail to take seriously the teaching of the Reformers as it would apply to the life of the church today. In particular, it would seem that we have failed to wrestle with their understanding of justification.

At this point I would like to explain the terminology that I use. The doctrine is properly called "justification by grace alone through faith alone." Through the years, a kind of shorthand has risen whereby we have spoken of "justification by faith alone." In and of itself this is innocent enough and it avoids having to keep repeating the full formula. But the trouble with this abbreviation is that it can give a quite mistaken view of what the doctrine is really saying. When "by grace alone" is dropped from the phrase the impression is given that faith is the primary element in justification. But then faith begins to appear as something that we must perform. And so, ironically, the term "justification by faith" leads to a new doctrine of works. Faith comes to be seen as a work that we must accomplish in order to save ourselves. A few years ago Will Herberg and other commentators noted that a predominant aspect of North American religion was that we have "faith in faith." To believe fervently is good regardless of what it is we believe. No doubt this attitude is partly the result of the abbreviation "by faith alone."

To insist upon speaking of justification by grace alone through faith alone is to make clear that the primary aspect of justification is not our faith but God's grace. Because God has acted for us in Jesus Christ, because God's love seeks us, because God forgives our sins, we are justified.

This gracious act and attitude of God is received by us
through faith, but it is not our faith that saves us, it is God's
grace alone. Luther notes how Paul united "by faith" with
"through Christ." Luther says that this is directed to those
who think that they can approach God independently of
what God has done in Christ. And so he emphasizes that it
is not just any faith that can save us but faith in Christ.[12]

The doctrine of justification cannot be understood unless
we see that it speaks of the God who has sought us and
seeks us before we think of seeking him. There has grown
up a widespread tendency in Protestantism whereby people
are heard to tell how "I have found Christ," which leads to
exhorting unbelievers "to find Christ." All of this makes it
sound as though Christ were hiding somewhere and it is up
to us to go out and locate him. Inevitably this gives the
impression that faith is a work that we do, and for which we
may take credit. Worse still, it leaves the impression that it
is Christ who is lost, not we. But when we speak of
justification by grace, we are reminded that while we were
yet sinners Christ died for us (Rom. 5:8). That is, before we
had the bright idea of looking for Christ, he was out looking
for us and had found us. If we love Christ, it is only because
he first loved us (I John 4:19).

Without claiming that all these perversions are the result
of the abbreviations "justification by faith alone" or "by
faith alone," it is apparent that the abbreviations encourage
the perversions. Hence, despite the extra space that it takes
to print out the doctrine in full, I shall use the longer form:
"justification by grace alone through faith alone." When,
for the sake of convenience, I try to save space I shall do it
by the simple abbreviation "justification." I hope this will
not be as open to misunderstanding as "justification by faith
alone."

II

The Nature of Righteousness

IN SPEAKING of justification by grace alone through faith alone, misunderstanding sometimes arises because the word "justification" is not understood. It is important, therefore, to begin by seeing that the translation of the Bible into English can use either the term "justification" or the term "righteousness." Thus in the key statement of Hab. 2:4 (quoted in Rom. 1:17) the King James Version reads, "The just shall live by his faith," whereas the Revised Standard Version reads, "The righteous shall live by his faith." Justification is making or being made righteous. In the Bible there is also the implication that justification means being made right in one's relationship to God or another person.

The doctrine of justification, therefore, can be understood only if we begin with the nature of righteousness as it is taught by Jesus. When we examine this we find that the doctrine of justification by grace alone through faith alone is not an accidental or peripheral doctrine in Christianity. It is required by the ideal and form of righteousness that Jesus held before his followers. Although there is good reason to argue that Jesus' view was a continuation of the Old Testament view, Jesus' teaching of righteousness brought him into sharp conflict with the teaching of the religious leaders of the time in which he lived.

Righteousness: External or Internal?

When the world speaks of a righteous person it is quite likely to think simply in terms of conduct. Righteousness is thus a quality of persons that can be judged by an observation of their behavior. For example, the law enforcement institutions of society are concerned with right behavior. They do not care why people obey the law, so long as they do obey it. The person who breaks no laws is righteous in their sight regardless of the motivation that produces the law-abiding behavior.

Behaviorism has been a popular theory in the twentieth century. Arising in psychology, it has been picked up by philosophers and others because behaviorist theories promise a neat and scientific way for studying human activities. The essence of behaviorism is that all meaningful or significant statements about human behavior can be made in terms of describing the observable physical behavior of human organisms. To speak of publicly unobservable events such as motivations, introspection, or emotional reactions is meaningless unless you can translate what is said into statements about bodily actions that can be publicly verified. For example, if we say that someone is feeling nervous, the statement would be meaningful to behaviorism only if we can point to some observable aspect of his body. We might thus justify the statement to behaviorists by counting the rate of his heartbeat, taking his blood pressure, or seeing him twiddle his fingers.

In the realm of ethics we may coin the term "ethical behaviorism" for the view which says that ethical statements refer exclusively to external, observable behavior. Ethical behaviorism would define righteousness exclusively in terms of what a person does or does not do. Ethical behaviorism, so defined, is closely linked to what has been known traditionally as legalism. Legalism defines righteousness in terms of the keeping of certain rules or laws of conduct. The religious establishment of Jesus' day was committed to ethical behaviorism. God had given his law to his people and the person who obeyed the law was righteous in the eyes of God. This attitude is pictured in Jesus' parable about the Pharisee and the publican (Luke 18:9–14). The Pharisee claims to be righteous on the basis of his behavior. He is not like other men who are extortioners, unjust, or adulterers, and he gives a tithe of all that he has. That is, his claim to virtue is purely a matter of his external and observable behavior without any hint of what goes on in his inner life. Whether or not he loves God is not mentioned. He obeys the law fully and completely; what more can be asked?

Jesus, however, broke radically from the ethical behaviorism of his time and place. In the Sermon on the Mount he noted that his hearers had been taught that they should not kill, but Jesus said that anyone who is angry with his brother is liable to judgment (Matt. 5:21–22). Similarly, while the law had forbidden adultery, Jesus said that "every one who looks at a woman lustfully has already committed adultery with her in his heart" (Matt. 5:28). In these teachings Jesus cuts through the outer behavior of a person and looks at what is in the inner self of the person. These must have been hard sayings to the legalists of Jesus' time. The law was neat and simple: it regulated all observable behavior— but who could regulate the inner workings of a person's mind?

Jesus surely did not mean these statements to be the cause of neurotic guilt complexes as they sometimes have been. There are times and places where anger rises naturally in the human heart and even Jesus felt anger on occasion (e.g., Mark 3:5). Similarly, because we are biological creatures, it is natural to have sexual feelings aroused by appropriate circumstances. If we begin to castigate ourselves for all feelings of anger or sexual interest, we would be rejecting the goodness of God's creation. It would appear that Jesus' meaning here is a simple one. He is insisting that righteousness is not simply a matter of what we do but is rather a question of why we do it.

Before an act of murder or adultery is committed, there has first been the motivation of the person involved. In his or her heart there has been a murderous anger or an adulterous lust. What Jesus seems to be saying is that many people may have the same motivations in their hearts without ever carrying out the external actions. There may be many reasons for not acting upon our motivations, but obviously one of the most common reasons is a fear of the consequences. The laws of all societies make it perilous to commit murder, and the laws or social pressures of all societies make it costly to commit adultery. Therefore when a person refrains from such actions it may not be a matter of the purity of the heart but simply a question of prudence. Jesus would appear to be saying that where the reason for not acting upon one's motivation or desires is a prudential or selfish one, the person is as unrighteous in God's eyes as the person who actually commits the crime.

This interpretation is borne out by Jesus' teachings in other contexts. When speaking of the practice of piety or the giving of alms, Jesus warns against doing such for the sake of being seen by others. Behavioristically judged, a person either does or does not pray, a person either does or does not give alms to the poor. But Jesus moves behind the external actions to ask why they are performed. If their motivation is the selfishly prudent one of establishing a public reputation, then the person performing them is not righteous in God's eyes (Matt. 6:1–6). To those who had

been successful in achieving a behavioristic righteousness,
Jesus said, "So you also outwardly appear righteous to men,
but within you are full of hypocrisy and iniquity" (Matt.
23:28). The point is clear: the outward rectitude of life is
made worthless by the motivations that lie behind it. Again,
when Jesus is asked why his disciples did not keep the
religious laws of fasting he replied: "Can the wedding guests
mourn as long as the bridegroom is with them? The days
will come, when the bridegroom is taken away from them,
and then they will fast." (Matt. 9:14–17.) In other words, an
action such as fasting is of no significance unless it is an
authentic expression of the inner feelings of a person. Jesus
emphasized that a person is not defiled by food or drink but
rather by what comes from the heart. "For out of the heart
come evil thoughts, murder, adultery, fornication, theft,
false witness, slander" (Matt. 15:19). Jesus used an analogy
for the ethical life of a good tree bearing good fruit.
Similarly, "The good man out of the good treasure of his
heart produces good" (Luke 6:45). Again there is emphasis
upon the inner motivation that lies behind the external
actions.

No one in the history of Christian thought has understood
Jesus' point about the inner motivation better than Martin
Luther. Luther's commentary on Romans emphasizes again
and again that the law of God cannot be fulfilled by external
obedience but only when the obedience is accompanied by
a loving, willing, and joyful heart. Thus he says, "Therefore
what is the qualitative difference between the man who
does evil and the man who wants to do evil, granted that he
does not do so because he is compelled by fear or lured by
the love of some temporal reward?" [13] Luther is affirming
that true righteousness is not a matter of doing or not doing
certain things, but in having the desire to do the good
without any prudential motivation. Thus Luther sees that

we are called to a selfless love of God. "But to love Him for the sake of His gifts or for some advantage is the lowest kind of love, that is, to love Him with a selfish desire. This is using God but not enjoying Him." [14] For Luther this leads to the ultimate conclusion that the mark of salvation is precisely that a person does not care about his own salvation but would, like Paul, be willing to give up his own salvation for the sake of others (see Rom. 9:3). So Luther can say: "But now no one knows whether he loves God with a pure heart unless he has experienced in himself that if it should please God he would not desire even to be saved nor would he refuse to be damned. For the damned suffer so severely because they are unwilling to be damned and do not resign themselves to this will of God, which they cannot do without the grace of God." [15] Nothing could be farther from an evangelism that tries to persuade us to be Christian because it would be good for us!

The point that true righteousness is more than a matter of external actions is recognized widely quite apart from Christian circles. People in general see that the ethical value of an action depends upon its motivation. After World War II the United States engaged in the most widespread relief program that the world has ever witnessed as billions of dollars were poured into foreign aid to help build or rehabilitate other nations. But the American people were shocked to find that their generosity won little in the way of gratitude. "Yankee Go Home" signs often seemed to be the typical result of massive efforts to aid other nations. Why was this? No doubt in part it was an expression of ingratitude and perversity, but the main reason was that the primary motivation of the foreign aid was no secret. American political leaders justified the foreign aid to their electorate by insisting that it was necessary to prevent the aided countries from going communist. So obvious was this that it became a worldwide joke that any country which could not get American aid should immediately organize a native communist movement so that it could become a candidate for aid. In other words, while the world recognizes that feeding the hungry and clothing the naked are good deeds, nonetheless, when they are done for self-seeking motives, they fall short of righteousness.

In a similar way during the 1960's many white persons who were proud of their liberal views on racial relations wore shocked to find that blacks saw them as among the chief enemies. Was this ungrateful perversity upon the part of the blacks? By no means! Although there were a number of reasons for the reaction, a basic reason was that the blacks resented being used by whites as a means to achieving status in certain quarters. The white person who rounds up a few token blacks or "takes an Indian to lunch" to demonstrate to himself and others that he or she is a good solid righteous person is insulting the minority group. It is a way of using others that is more cynical and hurts more than the open prejudice of an Archie Bunker.

Martin Luther saw this fact clearly. He notes how giving to those poorer than ourselves can be a source of considerable satisfaction to our own egos. "This gives much greater pleasure, obviously because of vainglory and boasting. For here 'it is more blessed to give than to receive!' (Acts 20:35.) They are like God Himself, but only in their pride." [16]

Righteousness in Relationship to God

Jesus' concern about the inner motivation of actions is no doubt related to the human insight that the goodness of a deed can be destroyed by the motivation that inspires it. But Jesus' thinking goes deeper. For Jesus, man's righteous-

ness is a matter of his relationship to God. It is significant
that Jesus' most typical term for God is not "king" and
certainly not "lawgiver"; it is, of course, "Father." In using
this term for God, Jesus was pointing to the personal
relationship which we may have with God. The basic
nature of this relationship is described by Jesus in another
radically personal term—love.

In taking these terms from normal human relationships,
Jesus did not simply say that God and the God-human
relationship are like what we already know in our human
relationships. On the contrary, in applying these terms to
the God-human relationship, he gave a new dimension to
our views of parenthood and love.

A classic expression of Jesus' concept of God and his love
is found in the parable of the prodigal son (Luke 15:11–32).
In this parable the son takes his inheritance into the far
country and wastes it in riotous living. The bitterness of his
older brother is typical of what we might expect in a human
family. The prodigal has made an ass of himself, wasted
his father's hard-earned money, and made his family a
laughing-stock, an object of the derision of respectable
people. If he is to be accepted back into the family, at
the very least he ought to be made to pay for what he has
done.

The prodigal himself understood the attitude of the elder
son. And so, when he was down on his luck in the far
country, he made up a pretty little speech whereby he
would confess that he had sinned against heaven and his
father and was no more worthy of being called a son. He
would ask simply to become a hired servant in his father's
house, no doubt hoping he could thereby earn his way back
into the good graces of his father. Having proven himself
capable of honest and fruitful labor, he could once more
hold up his head and perhaps even again be a son.

But the father never gave the son an opportunity to make the self-debasing speech or to suggest the bargain whereby he might earn his way back into the home. Instead, the father ran out to meet the son, embraced him, and announced a party to celebrate the occasion. This parable is one of the best descriptions of what justification by grace through faith really means.

At the center of the parable of the prodigal is the question of interpersonal relationships. The relationship between persons is meaningful only when it is a matter of free responses that arise from the heart. Thus at the beginning of the parable the father faces a choice. He is not compelled to give the inheritance to the son and probably the father understood his son well enough to know that once the boy was on his own with the money in his pocket, there would be trouble. No doubt the father's heart longed to prevent the problems that he could see hanging over his son's head. And it would have been easy to do so. The prodigal does not appear to have been the type who would have gone off without the means to pay his way. The father could very simply have refused to turn over the inheritance. But if he had taken that course he would not have had a son, he would have had a slave. The boy's behavior would have been externally much preferable to what happened in the far country, but he would have felt resentment against his father and he would have wasted his substance with harlots in his heart. In short, the father knew that the only hope of having a father-son relationship between himself and his son was to take the gamble of giving the son the inheritance. It might not work; the boy might forever leave the father and go his own way. But there was the chance that he would freely and willingly return to the father-son relationship. If, however, the father withheld the inheritance, there was no chance of maintaining a father-son relationship; instead, there would be a keeper-kept relationship.

The same principle is found at the end of the parable. There would be a great temptation for the father to feel that he must see that the wayward son had learned his lesson. The best way to do this would seem to be to accept the boy's bargain. He could be returned to the home as a hired servant. When he had paid back at least a part of the wasted inheritance and had demonstrated his responsibility, then he could be gradually returned to sonship. But, in fact, this method could not lead to the free interpersonal relations which the father sought to have with his son. The relationship of father and son would depend upon a legalistic system of payments. Who would decide at what point the son had repaid enough money or demonstrated his new responsibility sufficiently? Furthermore, there would be built into this relationship a continuous temptation for the son to masquerade a greater compliance with his father's wishes than in fact he felt. Since it would be to his own prudent interests to please the father, he would be continually tempted to hide his negative feelings and to pretend to have a righteousness that he did not feel. Only if the father freely accepted the son back home as a son without any ifs, ands, or buts could there be developed the fully free father-son relationship which the father desired. This might not succeed, because there are no guarantees in the realm of interpersonal relations.

We can speculate freely as to what happened after the return of the prodigal. Did he settle down to a harmonious relationship with his father? Perhaps; we like to think that he did. But it is quite possible that the son took his father's love for weakness and decided that he could henceforth work the old man for anything that he wanted. Quite possibly the resentments of the elder son were justified by the later behavior of the returned prodigal. We will never know.

Somewhere C. S. Lewis comments that he is surprised that the critics of God have brought almost every criticism against the character of God that could be imagined except the one for which there is some real evidence—namely, that God is an inveterate gambler. Certainly God, as pictured through Jesus' parable of the prodigal, is a gambler. But the goal of personal relationships which God is seeking with his children cannot be achieved in any other way. Although the free forgiveness of the father is a gamble that may not work, the alternatives are certain not to result in the relationship sought by the father, even though they may result in better external behavior.

Righteousness and the Law

When we begin from the fact that God seeks an interpersonal relationship with his children, we can see why the law cannot result in righteousness. Luther, summarizing Paul, says: "The works of the Law are those . . . which take place outside of faith and grace and are done at the urging of the Law, which either forces obedience through fear or allures us through the promise of temporal blessings. But the works of faith . . . are those which are done out of the spirit of liberty and solely for the love of God." [17] Because, by its very nature, the law compels, cajoles, or enforces behavior, it is incompatible with a free interpersonal relationship. A happy marriage, for example, cannot be maintained by the penalties involved in the marriage laws of the nation. Such laws may keep a man and wife together, but they cannot possibly give rise to the free expression of love which is necessary for a happy marriage.

When Luther says that the law "either forces obedience

through fear or allures us through the promise of temporal blessings," he is not giving simply a description of the law but also a definition. Wherever behavior is governed by an external power, or where the behavior is motivated by fear of consequences or promise of rewards, the "law" is present. The laws passed by governments, enforced by police, and sanctioned by penalties are obvious examples of law. But the laws passed by governments may not be nearly as demanding as the laws enforced by public opinion. We referred above to the legal sanctions surrounding marriage. However, the law, as it operates in the realm of marriage, appears in the form of public opinion more often than in the laws of the state today. Most modern nations have liberalized divorce laws so that the legal impediments to a divorce are more of a nuisance than a hindrance except among the poor. However, in some quarters divorce still carries considerable social stigma, and there is always a pride that is reluctant to make a public admission of failure in any major undertaking. In such ways the law may operate to keep a couple together quite apart from the laws of the state. The point is, however, that no matter what form the law takes, it cannot create a happy marriage. Only when husband and wife enter freely, willingly, and joyfully into loving interpersonal relationship will the marriage be a happy one.

In the light of Jesus' teachings about the nature of God and God's relationship to his children, it is clear that the law cannot establish such relationships any more than it can create a happy marriage. Since Biblical righteousness is defined in terms of the right relationship with God, it cannot be established by law. Behavior that is law-motivated is thus not righteous. This is why the Protestant Reformers opposed works-righteousness. Never were they opposed to the doing of good works as such. But when they preached justification by grace alone through faith alone, they were driving home the point that actions motivated by law could not bring about the interpersonal relationship which God sought with his children. Thus, in the quotation above, Luther contrasts the works of the law with the works of faith "which are done out of the spirit of liberty and solely for the love of God."

When we see that the Protestant doctrine of justification is based upon a concern for the motivation behind actions rather than with the actions themselves, we can see how many of the actions mentioned in the last chapter make it difficult for people to understand the Protestant teaching. Whenever the church backs various methods of compelling "right" behavior, it tends to give the impression that it is behavior, rather than motivation, that counts. When churches or Christians in the name of faith attempt to get the government to pass laws, they need to examine carefully whether or not such action may witness against the doctrine of justification.

Luther understood more profoundly than Calvin the limits of the state. The laws of the state are, by definition, law in the theological sense of the term. The state, as Luther put it, has the right to wield the sword and the sword thus stands as the symbol of the punishment that can motivate people to do that which they would not do if left to their own inner inclinations. Luther saw that the state could not bring about righteousness in people. Only God's Word could do that. Luther emphasized that there are two kingdoms in the world, the temporal kingdom (the state), which wields the sword, maintains law, order, and justice, and the heavenly kingdom, which preaches the Word and thus moves people to love of God. The Christian, said Luther, must distinguish carefully between these two kingdoms. The state must not be used to try to impose that which only God's word can accomplish. "Therefore, where the temporal authority presumes to prescribe laws for the soul, it encroaches upon God's government and only misleads souls and destroys them." [18]

Righteousness and Legislation

This principle of Luther's has far-reaching implications. As Luther himself saw, this meant that the state should not attempt to legislate orthodox belief. Such laws cannot please God, because "he desires that our faith be based simply and entirely on his divine word alone." [19] But we can go farther: the state should not attempt to legislate behavior that ought to be the fruit of the gospel. There was a time when governments, even in Protestant countries, passed laws to enforce attendance at worship services. This is a glaring contradiction of Luther's principles and most Protestants today would agree. But we do not always see so clearly that other aspects of Christian behavior cannot be legitimately legislated.

If all people had pure faith, Luther believed, there would be no need for the state nor for the sword. But Luther also recognized that only a minority have faith and even they are both justified and sinners at the same time. The state is thus necessary to restrain the evil machinations of the wicked. At first sight it would seem that Luther has a purely negative view of the state, that it is simply the dike against sin. It maintains sufficient law and order so that a relatively decent life can be lived and so that the gospel can be preached. But Luther does have a more positive view of what the state can do. Raising the question of why the Christian should support the state, Luther answers that we do so because of love of the neighbor. Even though the Christian may feel no need of the state for his personal life, "nevertheless, he concerns himself about what is serviceable and of benefit to others." [20] This means that the Christian should look to the state not simply to restrain the lawless and prevent murder and robbery; the state should also seek justice and protect the weak from the strong. Paul Tillich used to tell his classes that it was no accident that the Lutheran countries had been pioneers in developing the welfare state. This was in keeping with Luther's concept of using the state to express love to the neighbor.

The record of Protestant churches in the modern world, however, has not been in harmony with Luther's understanding of the state's place. By and large, Protestant churches have not been in the forefront of seeking legislation from governments to protect the weak. With some notable exceptions, particularly during the 1960's, Protestant churches have accepted the *status quo,* with its built-in discrimination against the poor in general and minority groups in particular. However, these churches have established a reputation for advocating legislation to restrict the personal conduct of people. Prohibition still stands as one of the major political triumphs of Protestantism in North America. It surprises no one to hear that churches are fighting for censorship of movies or magazines, for stricter laws against the nonmedical use of drugs, and against liberalization of laws on divorce, homosexuality, or abortion.

Recently on a television panel show, a participant spoke of the "Anglo-Saxon, Judeo-Christian" ethical attitude, which has encouraged our population to stand in continual judgment over the actions of other people. When such a statement is made, one wants to rise up and protest that it entirely misses the central themes of the Judeo-Christian Scriptures: mercy, forgiveness, and love. But one also has to confess that the record of the churches has done much to justify the making of such a sweeping judgment. When churches so consistently come out for legal restrictions upon personal conduct they give the impression that they have set themselves up to judge the conduct of others and believe that they can enforce righteousness in others by the passing of laws.

I have recently witnessed an interesting illustration of the concern to enforce righteous behavior without regard for the underlying motivation. I have been a member of a committee set up by our Provincial Government to study the question of how "family planning" could be encouraged in our Province. Alarmed by the rapid rise in illegitimate births and legal abortions, the Government was concerned to see what could be done to decrease the number of unwanted pregnancies. One of the first steps of our committee was to analyze the statistics on abortions and illegitimate births. This revealed that both occurred most frequently among unmarried teen-agers. Thus it appeared to the committee that a major problem was that of getting information to this group about how to prevent pregnancy. Immediately, however, some members of the committee pointed out that this would bring the condemnation of the churches upon our heads. We would be charged with condoning premarital sexual relationships and, by removing the fear of pregnancies, we would be encouraging premarital sex. The past record of the churches had given rise to the expectation of such a reaction. When reaction from the churches began to come in, it confirmed the warnings made by the committee members.

What does it say to people when the churches are identified with this kind of reaction? Obviously it says that churches are institutions that are concerned to regulate proper behavior at all costs. They would be willing to see the continuance of the tragedies of abortions and illegitimate births rather than to lose the deterring power inherent in the fear of these tragedies. This means that the church is seen as being primarily concerned with behavioristic ethics rather than with the underlying motivations of people and why they do or do not engage in certain actions.

When laws that regulate personal behavior are under discussion, it is sometimes said that "you cannot legislate morality." But this phrase is somewhat ambiguous, as is evident when it is answered that most laws do legislate morality. Laws against murder legislate the morality that proclaims, "Thou shalt not kill." Laws to prohibit discrimination upon the basis of race, creed, sex, or nationality are examples of legislating the morality of the just treatment of people. Therefore, it is concluded that if someone believes in laws to prohibit racial discrimination in employment, he should have no reason for arguing against laws to censor movies on the basis that you cannot legislate morality. Because the term "morality" is broad enough to apply to all areas of human action, there is a real sense in which most laws can be considered to legislate morality. The phrase has not located the real problem.

A better way of locating the problem is to speak of those laws which create a crime where there is no victim. A law against discrimination in employment practices is a law that protects the victim of discrimination. Such a law is fully in keeping with Luther's point that the Christian should use the power of the state to protect the weak from the strong and thus to maintain justice. But when the law makes it a crime to smoke marijuana, there is no victim. If, in fact, smoking marijuana is injurious to the health, the person is harming only himself. Similarly, homosexual acts between "consenting adults" have no victims. Therefore laws that prohibit such homosexual acts are quite different from laws that protect minority groups from the discrimination of the majority.

From a theological point of view, it is important to make

a clear distinction between laws that protect people from those who would injure them and laws that seek to protect people from themselves. Because the power of different groups within society is widely different, it is imperative that the power of the state should be brought to bear on behalf of the weak who cannot protect themselves against the predatory aggressions of those who are stronger. Christian love for the neighbor should move us to seek such laws from the government. In such cases it is clear that the concern is to protect the potential victims. The laws are not passed in order to make the aggressors more righteous but simply to restrain their aggression. A law against the monopoly practices of industry is not passed to make industrial management more righteous, it is passed to protect the public from practices that would be harmful to it. But when a law is passed to make a crime where there is no victim and thus a person is being protected from himself, it would appear that the only purpose of the law is to make people righteous within themselves. When churches seek the passage of such laws they are announcing to one and all that their primary concern is with a purely behavioristic righteousness.

Of course, the question of crimes without victims is not always a clear one. Many people who argue for laws against pornography are firmly convinced that pornography does produce victims. It stimulates sexual crimes, and so on. However, it would appear that, insofar as we have concrete evidence on this question, there is little scientific support for this position. Where pornography has been legalized, as in Denmark, it seems to have resulted in a drop in sexual crimes. The evidence is not so strong that we should start campaigns to encourage pornography to protect the victims of sex crimes. But, given the present weight of the evidence, if the churches press for laws against pornography, they perpetuate the impression that their real concern is to legislate personal behavior and that thus they believe that external behavior alone constitutes true righteousness.

If the churches have acted in the political realm so as to give the impression that they are champions of a behavioristic view of ethics, they have reinforced this by their activity in institutions under their control. As noted in the last chapter, what distinguishes the Christian college or other institution from a secular one of the same nature is all too often a stricter set of rules and regulations to legislate the conduct of persons. This too is a case of the use of the "law" in Luther's sense. Students in the Christian college are compelled under threat of expulsion or other penalties to act in certain "Christian" ways regardless of how they may feel inclined to act.

The doctrine of justification is rooted in the fact that Jesus' mission made him the friend of sinners. From this we might suppose that Christian institutions, be they schools, hospitals, missions to the poor, or otherwise, would be marked by a greater willingness to provide a place for sinners than would be found in similar secular institutions. And sometimes this is what is found. In such cases, it is recognized that those who are branded as the more flagrantly sinful are precisely the ones who need most the support and influence of the Christian community. Only through such support and influence, it is recognized, can there be brought about a radical change in the inner motivation of such persons. But all too often, it must be confessed, Christian institutions are quicker in expelling such "evil influences" than are secular ones. This gives the impression that the institution is concerned only with external behavior, and where the law cannot enforce such behavior, the offender must be ruthlessly expelled.

Whenever the churches are ready to resort to law, either the law of the state or rules within their own institutions, they make it difficult for people to believe that they stand for an inner righteousness. They appear to be concerned only with the determination to regulate external conduct according to certain rules and regulations. As a result, their preaching of justification seems strange and unconvincing. If the heart of justification lies in the kind of righteousness that Jesus preached, then the preoccupation of the churches with compelling a behavioristic form of righteousness is an inevitable hindrance that keeps people from understanding the gospel of justification preached in the churches.

Because the practice of Protestant churches has done so much to undermine their teaching of justification, it seems important at this stage to try to examine why such practice has been so widespread. I shall devote the next chapter to an analysis of the underlying reasons why Protestant churches have felt called to be so concerned with a purely behavioristic view of righteousness.

III

Justification and Religious Paternalism

THE DOCTRINE of justification, I have argued, presupposes that true righteousness involves the joyful willingness of the heart. This righteousness cannot result from laws enforced by penalties or activities that are stimulated by rewards. But the activities of Protestant churches have helped to give the impression that Christianity is primarily concerned with legislating good behavior. This results in a credibility gap when we preach justification since our actions speak more loudly than our words. It is my thesis that this situation has arisen from out of a tension within historic Christianity between viewing Christianity as a prophetic Biblical faith and viewing it as a civil religion.

Civil Religion

The struggle between prophetic and civil religion appears in the Bible itself and persists through the whole history of the church. Rosemary Ruether describes a crucial point in the history of this tension when she says: "The ambiguity and tragedy of Christianity are that it is a faith with roots in revolutionary messianic hope, which, nevertheless, was co-opted into the imperialistic ideology and social structure of the later Roman Empire. Consequently, a culture and a

society originally antithetical to the messianic hope of
Judaism, from whose loins Christianity had sprung, became
the historical vehicle of the Church, and Christianity itself
was used to sanctify and perpetuate the hierarchical society
and world view of classical culture." [21] Ms. Ruether is
pointing to the time when Christianity became the official
religion of the Roman Empire and thus the civil religion of
Rome. To understand the significance of this we need to
see that every society seeks to develop a civil religion.
Therefore, wherever Christianity becomes the majority
religion of a society it will be faced with pressures to
become the civil religion of that culture. Protestant
churches may pride themselves upon having discarded more
of the patterns of ancient Rome than Ms. Ruether finds to
be the case in Roman Catholicism. But, in fact, this has
often meant no more than that they have become better
adapted to be the civil religion of the culture in which they
find themselves.

During the 1950's in North America there was a remarka-
ble revival of religion. A number of analysts of this
phenomenon, such as Will Herberg, Martin Marty, and A.
Roy Eckardt, pointed out that it was not a revival of
Christian or Jewish faith but a revival of "American
religion." [22] It was based upon a glorification of the
American way of life and closely related to the defense of
American ideals against the threat of "godless communism."
This American civil religion operated in and through the
traditional religious institutions of the nation. Although it
had Roman Catholic and Jewish wings, it remained in many
ways a Protestant phenomenon. What was happening was
that Protestantism was being used by American culture
even as Rome had used the church many centuries earlier.

Civil religion developed from the time when human
beings found themselves in the world and began to build

societies. Ants, bees, and other forms of life have inherited an internal code of conduct that governs their social behavior under all circumstances. Men and women, however, are not programmed in this way. As a result, whereas the social life of the beehive or anthill has remained static through the centuries, the human race has spawned an incredible number of social orders and moral codes. Each society has been built, to some degree, in defiance of its natural environment. Food, shelter, and protection had to be wrested from an environment that was seldom completely friendly. Furthermore, neighboring societies were usually a threat. It became a matter of life and death for the people that the rules and order of their society should have the obedience and unquestioned loyalty of the whole population. And so it is not surprising to find that a civil religion develops in every society. Religion becomes that scheme of meaning which gives a higher, usually divine, sanction to the structures of the society in question. Peter Berger has coined the apt phrase "a sacred canopy" to describe how religion acts as a protector of the ideals of a society. The pattern of behavior required by the society comes to be justified not because of its prudential or survival value but because it is the will of the gods or because it corresponds to the ultimate reality pattern of the universe.

Because people look to their religion as a sacred canopy over their way of life, religious leaders are expected to uphold "law and order." When the state supports a church or even when it grants tax privileges to all churches, it is not because it hopes that churches will offer a prophetic critique of society and its goals or ways. During the 1960's in the United States the clergy were often to be found marching in demonstrations against the racial injustices of the land and protesting the immorality of the war in

Vietnam. It was not surprising that we often heard threats that the tax privileges of the churches would be withdrawn if such acts continued. Obviously such religious leaders were not providing a sacred canopy to bless the actions of the nation. Why should churches receive tax concessions from a government whose policies they were attacking? On the other hand, a number of the religious leaders at this time were seriously wondering if the tax concessions were not an albatross around the neck of the church that kept it from being faithful to its Lord.

As we examine the history of religion we find that it has generally been a conservative force in society. This is not surprising since one of the primary reasons for religion is the desire for a transcendent framework of justification for the *status quo.* The mores of each society are seen by its members as the ultimate form of morality. Since religion is the guardian of this morality, society expects religious persons and institutions to support the society as it is. There is room, of course, for religion to condemn deviants from the social norm even when the deviants appear in high places. But it is not expected that religion will question the validity of the norm itself. Because religious institutions are expected to support the ultimate values and goals of the society, religious institutions come to see themselves as the guardians of the public morality. This takes the form of preaching, teaching, and passing resolutions that are supportive of society's values and goals. Almost inevitably this leads to the view that the religious people have a responsibility for the behavior of all persons in the society. In a Judeo-Christian context this has taken form in the almost universal belief that we are called to be our "brother's keeper." The phrase, of course, comes from Gen. 4:9, where Cain uses it. Because it is so popular to affirm that the essence of Christianity is to be our brother's keeper, we need to take a close look at what the Genesis story actually says.

Cain, having killed his brother, Abel, out of jealousy, was confronted by God, who asked him where his brother was. Cain replied, "I do not know; am I my brother's keeper?" Because Cain was condemned by God, it may seem that he was condemned for failing to be his brother's keeper, but that misses the point of the story. Cain, caught in his guilt by God, did what we all do, he tried to bluff his way out. When asked where his brother was, he dared not answer the truth. So he said that he did not know, and to justify himself he asked God if he was supposed to be his brother's keeper. Under most circumstances this would be a perfectly legitimate answer. Abel was a mature adult and Cain was not supposed to keep him on a leash. Abel was free to come and go as he pleased without asking Cain's permission, so there was no reason, under normal circumstances, why Cain should know where Abel was. But these were not normal circumstances. Cain had killed Abel and he was condemned not because he had failed as Abel's keeper but because he had failed as a brother and a human being. "The voice of your brother's blood is crying to me from the ground" (Gen. 4:10).

Even a casual reading of Gen., ch. 4, should indicate that it does not teach that we are to be our brother's "keeper." Yet it remains one of the firmest ideas in our society that we are called to be keepers of our brother. Again and again I have found that when I have tried to explain to church groups that we are not meant to be our brother's keeper, I have been met with indignant skepticism and I have been accused of betraying a fundamental article of our faith.

The Shorter Oxford English Dictionary gives some interesting definitions of the word "keeper." Among other things it says: "One who has charge, care, or oversight of

any person or thing. . . . One who keeps a mistress. . . .
Any mechanical device for keeping something in its place."
This is a significant set of definitions. The very idea of a
keeper implies superiority and control. If I am my brother's
keeper, then I have a position of superiority over him, he is
in my charge, I am called to keep him in his place. It is
interesting to ask people to evaluate being their brother's
keeper in the light of the Golden Rule, which admonishes us
to do unto others as we would have them do to us. Not
many of us want to be kept; we resent it when others
attempt to "keep us in our place," tell us what we may do,
and generally restrict our freedom to be ourselves. Yet we
still want to be our brother's keeper.

Often people defend their use of the term "keeper" by
saying that they do not mean by it what the dictionary says.
To be my brother's keeper, they say, means simply that I am
to be concerned with his welfare, ready to aid him in time
of need and to help to bear his burdens. But if that is what
we mean, why do we keep using the term "keeper" with all
its connotations of superiority and paternalism? If we want
to express this kind of concern, we could do so by speaking
of being our brother's brother or our sister's sister. These
terms carry the connotations of love, concern, and willingness to help without the implications of superior-inferior
relationships that are found in the term "keeper." I do not
think that it is an accident that we use so glibly and easily
the term "keeper." Behind the use of this word lies the
view that the religious institutions and religious people are
divinely commissioned to uphold public rectitude. The
religious people are in a position of moral superiority and
thus have a duty to see that the lesser breeds without the
law are made to behave themselves. So it is necessary to
pass rigorous legislation to keep people living up to the
standards protected by religion. Behind the theme of being

our brother's keeper lies the presupposition that religion is
called to play a paternalistic role in society.

Prophetic Religion

While religion has tended to be a conservative defense of
the *status quo* and has tended to be the paternalistic keeper
of those who would break the codes of society, the Biblical
faith presents another view of religion. The Bible is
centered on those prophets who stood against the stream of
their society and dared to condemn its ways. These
prophets usually had to bring their words of judgment
against the society in general.

In I Kings 22:2–38 there is a fascinating story that
illustrates the tension between civil and prophetic religion.
In this story the kings of Israel and Judah, Ahab and
Jehoshaphat, were planning an aggressive war to wrest the
city of Ramoth-gilcad from the control of Syria. Before
going to war, however, they desired the sacred canopy of
religion to cover and bless their plans. Four hundred
religious prophets gladly stepped forward to proclaim that
God blessed their plan and would bring them victory. But
Jehoshaphat asked for one more prophet and Ahab reluc-
tantly allowed Micaiah to speak, although he predicted that
Micaiah would not say anything good about him. Micaiah
saw the scheme for what it was, and said that if they went
forward with it, their armies would be defeated and King
Ahab would be killed. Micaiah was thrown into prison for
his words, while the kings went out to battle. They were
defeated and Ahab was killed as Micaiah had prophesied.

Reinhold Niebuhr once preached a sermon on this
passage, to which he gave the title "Four Hundred to
One." [23] The point of the title is that the false prophets
outnumbered the true prophet by four hundred to one.

Niebuhr wryly comments, "Perhaps the percentage of pure prophecy is not much higher even today." [24] Niebuhr's estimate may be on the pessimistic side, but his point is well taken. The official representatives of religion have usually been more concerned with preserving the community's standards than with being a means whereby the transcendence of God might be shown forth in judgment over the standards by which the society is run. This does not mean that inevitably the one is correct and the four hundred are wrong. Preachers cannot comfort themselves with a logic which says: Prophets were unpopular, I am unpopular, therefore I am a prophet. But the fact remains that if the world has nothing to say against us, God may have little to say for us. A true prophet can expect to be unpopular (Matt. 5:11–12).

The faith of Judaism, as found in the Old Testament, was built primarily upon its prophets, and the prophets were never the keepers of the public morality. Their works of judgment were seldom directed at those who fell below the community standards, and never could their words be interpreted as a canopy to bless the *status quo*. On the contrary, their words of judgment were directed primarily at the rich and the powerful who ruled and set the standards for their society (e.g., Isa. 10:1–2; 34:1–2; Jer. 5:26–29; Amos 4:1–3; Micah 2:1–2). They looked for a "Day of the Lord" that would come, not as a fulfillment, but as a destruction of the social order of their time and place (e.g., Isa. 10:3; Amos 5:18; Micah 3:9–12).

As we examine the life and teachings of Jesus, it is obvious that he was in the line of Micaiah and the great Old Testament prophets. In no way could he be considered a keeper of the standards of his society. The fact that the religious and political establishments of his society united to crucify him is evidence for this.

In John 12:47, Jesus says, "I did not come to judge the world but to save the world." These words, which are consistent with all of Jesus' life and teaching, separate him from the attitude of being a keeper of the society's morals. It is imperative that the keeper of the brethren should be quick to speak words of judgment when the wayward brothers step out of line. In religious circles this leads to what Dietrich Bonhoeffer described vividly as "priestly snuffing around in the sins of men in order to catch them out." [25] It is the attitude that causes people to act unnaturally pious in the presence of a clergyman. After all, clergymen are known as the keepers of public morality, so one must not open himself to their judgmental tendencies by speaking or acting as one would normally do.

Jesus was not judgmental in his relationship to people. On the contrary, he was known as the friend of sinners. He shocked the religious leaders by his practice of mixing and even eating with sinners (Matt. 9:10; 11:19; Mark 2:15–16; Luke 15:1–2). In the customs of the time, eating with a person was the ultimate expression of acceptance. It bound the persons together in a harmony of fellowship and expressed social and religious equality. In the eyes of the religious leaders, Jesus' practice of eating with sinners was a betrayal of his duty as a rabbi to uphold the moral standards of the community. Because Jesus was not standing in judgment over these sinners, it seemed that he was condoning their antisocial ways. He was failing to be his brother's keeper. He was wiping out the necessary distinction between the good and evil members of society and encouraging the evil to think of themselves as being as good as those elected to keep them in line.

Several of Jesus' teachings are directed to the criticisms that were made of his friendship for sinners. The famous chapter fifteen of Luke includes the parables of the lost sheep, the lost coin, and the lost (prodigal) son. Each of these parables teaches that God is primarily concerned to recover the lost. As a shepherd leaves ninety-nine sheep in the fold to look for one that is lost, or as a woman devotes all her energies to discover her one lost coin, so the God revealed in Jesus seeks his children who have gone astray. And as the father forgives his returning son, so God offers forgiveness to his prodigal children. These three parables form an important unity. Taken by itself, the parable of the prodigal son might not be too distasteful to those who see religion as the keeper of public morality. Such persons are not opposed to accepting the repentant back into the good graces of the righteous community. The reformed sinner can be an important exhibit in a religion viewed as the sacred canopy over society's morality. While the father in the parable might seem to be unduly generous, the principle could be acceptable. But the parable of the prodigal is preceded by two parables that picture God as actively seeking sinners to win them back. Instead of condemning the wayward, God so loved them that he went looking for them. This was shocking to the religious leadership of Jesus' day, and it remains a difficult theme wherever religion is seen as the guardian of public morality. Jesus made the same point again when he proclaimed that his task was not to call the righteous but the sinners, and that he had come to heal the sick, not those who were well (Matt. 9:12–13).

When religion sees itself as the protector of public morality, the keeper of its brother, it must become preoccupied with right behavior. Those who break the moral code of society are sinners; they must be condemned, punished, and forced into line. Only when this is done will the social structure be safe from the pagan emotions that seethe beneath its surface and threaten to bring destruction upon it. Religion, as the protector of the social fabric, must not do anything that would appear to condone sin. Religion must condemn sin wherever it is found and it must see that sinners are ostracized from the company of the righteous. It is a fine point of worldly wisdom that we should avoid evil companions because evil companions may lead us astray and certainly if we allow them in our company it will appear that we are condoning their behavior.

The life of Jesus seems to have been totally free of all of these attitudes. He was not primarily concerned with the external behavior of people; he was concerned with them as persons and with their inner state of being, as we saw in the last chapter. He did not fear for his reputation in mixing with evil companions, and obviously he did not feel that their influence would lead him astray. Jesus was ready to gamble on winning the sinners to true righteousness even at the expense of the social order. Instead of trying to be the keeper of sinners by imposing upon them condemnations or laws that would force upon them good behavior, he took the gamble of justification by grace alone through faith alone in order that they might be won to the true righteousness of relationship with their heavenly Father.

Jesus' Transcendence of Civil Religion

There are two incidents in John's Gospel which illustrate Jesus' attitudes at this point and which bear out John's report that Jesus said he had come not to judge the world but to save it. The first is the story of Jesus and the Samaritan woman (John 4:7–26). Jesus asks her for a drink, and this surprises her because it was not normal for a Jew to associate with the despised Samaritans. But Jesus ignores the racial differences and begins to reveal his messiahship to the woman. As she responds to his teaching, Jesus asks her to call her husband. When she says that she has no husband, Jesus agrees and tells her that she has had five husbands and is now living with a man to whom she is not married. If Jesus were the keeper of public morality, this revelation of his knowledge would have been used to try to drive her to a sense of guilt and repentance, but both Jesus and the woman ignore the moral implications of her common-law relationship. The purpose of Jesus' statements seems to be simply to give evidence of his messiahship, and that is precisely how the woman accepts them. She shows no sense of guilt for her lack of a marriage license but is impressed by this evidence that Jesus is a prophet. She goes back to tell the people of the village about the one who had been able to tell all about her past life.

The remarkable thing about this story is that Jesus is totally unconcerned with upholding the social institution of marriage. He presents himself to the woman as the Messiah and invites her to drink of the "living water" without any conditions. Unlike civil religion, Jesus does not say to the woman that if she will first clean up her illegitimate marital situation, she may taste of the living water. To the defender of civil religion, Jesus' behavior on this occasion must appear as undermining the public morality of marriage. Jesus is concerned only that the woman might "worship the Father in spirit and truth" and implies that such worship does not have as its prerequisite that she first become respectable in her personal life.

The second story is found in John 7:53 to 8:11—the story of the woman who had been caught in adultery. In some versions of the Bible, including the first edition of the RSV New Testament, this passage appears as a footnote and it is pointed out that whereas some Biblical manuscripts have it here (i.e., after John 7:52), in other manuscripts it is found after Luke 21:38, and in some manuscripts it does not appear at all. It is what scholars call a "floating tradition," inasmuch as it does not have any set position in the manuscripts that have come down to us. With this kind of dubious textual basis, have we any right to take the story seriously as an authentic historical account of Jesus? I believe that we do.

Faced with the fact that this passage appears in different places in various manuscripts but is totally absent from others, we must ask what theory best explains this fact. It is extremely difficult to believe that any scribe or copier of the manuscripts would have had the temerity to invent this story and add it to Sacred Scripture. But if the story is an authentic account of an event in the life of Jesus, it is not at all difficult to see how some copyist would find the story too dangerous to pass on. In other words, it is easy to see how the religious leadership, very conscious of its duty to uphold public morality, would feel justified in censoring out this story from the manuscripts, but it is almost totally impossible to imagine that same leadership inventing such a story to add to the Gospels. The story is in keeping with the teaching and character of Jesus as we see him in the four Gospels. Therefore, it would appear likely that the textual problems of this passage are themselves an illustration of the tension between civil religion and the prophetic spirit.

According to the story, the scribes and Pharisees brought to Jesus a woman who had been caught in adultery. Adultery was forbidden in the Ten Commandments, and in Lev. 20:10 the death penalty was prescribed for it. Since in this case the accusers demanded death by stoning, it would appear that the appeal was to Deut. 22:23–24, which sets stoning as the penalty for a betrothed virgin who has sexual intercourse with someone other than her intended husband.

The scribes and Pharisees did not bring the girl to Jesus simply for the sake of justice. It was one of a long series of incidents in which the religious leaders tried to catch Jesus

between the Scylla of Roman law and the Charybdis of
Jewish law. Rome did not allow the Jews the right to
practice capital punishment, so if Jesus advocated the
following of Jewish law he would be guilty of advocating
murder under the Roman law. On the other hand, if he did
not advocate stoning, he could be charged with opposing
Jewish law.

Adultery raises more issues than that of Roman vs. Jewish
law. Every society has had to protect marriage for the sake
of the social structure. Adultery has been viewed as a crime
in all cultures, even though the definition of adultery varies
with the form that marriage takes in different societies.
Religion, as the sacred canopy over the social structures, has
always taken a strong stand against adultery. It is significant, but not surprising, that although we are told that the
woman had been caught in the act of adultery, the accusers
did not bring the man to be executed. The Old Testament
law prescribed death for both participants in the act of
adultery, but society and its religious keepers have always
tended to look more severely upon the woman than upon
the man in such situations.

What were Jesus' options? He might have upheld Jewish
law by condemning the woman and saying that she
deserved death, but since the Jews did not have the power
to execute her, some other penalty would have to be
invoked. That would have avoided the trap set by the
religious leaders by upholding the sanctity of marriage
without alienating the Romans. But Jesus acted in a
radically different manner. For a time he seemed to pay
little attention to the tempters as he wrote in the sand.
When he spoke, he said, "Let him who is without sin among
you be the first to throw a stone at her."

Jesus' words at this point bring out what seems implicit in
all of his teaching about judging others. He warned people

not to judge lest they be judged with the same judgment that they meted out to others (Matt. 7:1–2). This was a subtle reminder to the would-be judge that his or her hands were never really clean. Also it said that those who choose to live under the law cannot escape being judged by the law. Jesus ridiculed those who became concerned about splinters in the eyes of others when they had planks in their own eyes (Luke 6:42). When he said that he had come to call sinners, not the righteous (Matt. 9:13), or when he said that it was the sick, not the well, who need a physician (Matt. 9:12), he was not saying that there are some persons in society who are righteous and well and have no need of God's forgiving grace. On the contrary, he was attempting to bring his self-righteous critics to their own need. In Luke 7:36–50 it is related that Jesus was eating at the house of a Pharisee when a woman of the street came to anoint him. The Pharisee was shocked that Jesus should let this sinful woman so treat him in public. Jesus rebuked him by pointing out how much more love the woman had bestowed upon him than the Pharisee had and concluded, "He who is forgiven little, loves little" (Luke 7:47). The implication is clear—the woman, conscious of her sinful condition, loves the one who represents forgiveness, but the Pharisee, wrapped securely in his own righteousness, sees no need to be forgiven and thus thinks he can afford to be judgmental of others and unloving.

Thus, in the story of the woman caught in adultery, Jesus' words about casting the first stone were effective. Slowly the accusers one by one withdrew. Were their hearts really touched by Jesus' words so that, looking into themselves, they knew that they were unworthy to cast the first stone? Or was it simply that none of them dared to be the first to flaunt the law of Rome? We cannot say. But the meaning of the rest of the story is clear.

Left alone with the woman, Jesus asks, "Has no one condemned you?" and when the woman replies, "No one, Lord," Jesus says, "Neither do I condemn you; go, and do not sin again." Here surely is the reason that the story has had difficulty in remaining in the Gospel manuscripts. Jesus clearly says that he does not condemn the woman. In the minds of those who see religion as the keeper of public morality, this would sound as though Jesus were condoning adultery. What will happen to the fabric of public morality if this story is allowed to be read? Would it not be safer to protect people from the dangerous implications of the story? Those who saw themselves as their brother's keeper would be gravely tempted to protect their weaker brethren from the perilous implication of the story by simply dropping it from the record. It is, therefore, not surprising that the story is missing from many manuscripts. The surprising thing is that so many manuscripts included it.

Is Jesus, in fact, condoning adultery? A close look at the story does not indicate this to be the case. Jesus sends the woman away with the admonition not to sin again. But what is evident is Jesus' real concern for the woman as a person. He was not afraid of whether his actions would encourage immorality; he was primarily concerned for the woman to be a changed person. Condemning her for her actions could not achieve that purpose. The keepers of their brethren would at the very least have sent the woman away with words such as: All right, you can go this time, but see that it does not happen again because next time I will let them stone you. If the sacred canopy is to be kept over the social structures, surely there must be a warning that there is a limit to mercy and forgiveness. Even as a suspended sentence in a court of law combines mercy with upholding the dignity of the law, so such parting words would combine the divine sanction against adultery with the mercy exercised in this incident.

Jesus did not say those words. His purpose, as we have argued, was to establish a new spirit of righteousness in the person. The spirit that Jesus sought could not come as the result of threats. It could well be that words of warning would have had a drastic effect upon the future behavior of the woman. Face to face with the possibility of being stoned, she had undergone a traumatic experience. Going out, warned that mercy would not again be applied, she might well have lived a most rigorously moral life. But why? She would have been motivated by fear. In her heart she could remain an adulteress, even as she lived an outer life of unquestioned rectitude. Jesus surely knew enough of what is called "modern psychology" to know that in all probability this woman would henceforth be in the forefront of those who would be ready to stone anyone else who was guilty of adultery. Since fear would keep her from what she desired, she would not look kindly upon those who went where she feared to tread. No matter how effective threats might be in changing her behavior, threats could not lead her to the righteousness that Jesus sought for all men and women. That could come only if the woman received full and free forgiveness.

As was said in the last chapter, this is a gamble. What was the future of the woman? We do not know. We would like to think that Jesus' treatment of her led to real repentance and a new life. It is pleasant to suppose that this woman was Mary Magdalene or the woman who came to anoint Jesus in the house of the Pharisee. But it is quite possible that this woman breathed a sigh of relief when she left Jesus, laughed at his "weakness" behind his back, and resolved henceforth to exercise more care so that she would not be caught again. There is a third possibility. Perhaps the woman returned to her adultery but, as time passed, she meditated on her meeting with Jesus and later may have been moved to a new way of life. The way of justification is seldom as quickly effective in changing behavior as the way of retribution. That is one reason that religion, as the guardian of public morality, turns so readily to laws that "have teeth in them." But, although Jesus' action was a gamble from the point of view of the later behavior of the woman, it was the only possible course of action that could lead to Jesus' primary purpose of winning people to a joyous embracing of righteousness. Jesus was ready, therefore, to run the risk of appearing to undermine the public morality.

This is not to say that Jesus had no concern with public morality. Jesus had no desire to undermine the institution of marriage since he set a high ideal for marriage as a permanent relationship between a man and a woman. Marriage was intended by God in his creation of the human race (Mark 10:6–9). The ideal of marriage was a permanent relationship between the married partners. Thus divorce was granted only as a sort of afterthought because of the hardness of people's hearts (Mark 10:3–5). In fact, Jesus' words on marriage set a higher ideal than was common among either the Jews or the Gentiles of his time. But obviously he did not think that this ideal could be maintained by external laws or social pressures. The seemingly dangerous gamble that Jesus took with the institution of marriage when he refused to condemn either the adulteress or the Samaritan woman was, in reality, a greater support of marriage than it would have been had he ordered that both women be properly punished.

In the last chapter it was maintained that the church's practice in seeking governmental laws to regulate personal behavior has resulted in undermining its teaching of justification. This chapter tries to show why this practice has been so widespread. When the church accepts the role of being the civil religion and takes responsibility for the public morality, it easily leads to the view that the church must work for legislation to uphold morality. In North America civil religion has always tended to the view that if we did not have legislation against something we would be condoning it. Thus Christians insist that we must not remove laws against prostitution, gambling, abortion, pornography, and the like even though we know that such laws are not effective in preventing these practices. If the laws should be removed, we are told, it would amount to condoning these actions. So the laws remain on the books and provide a golden opportunity for organized crime to move into these areas.

The determination of the churches to keep such laws reveals the degree to which we have let civil religion replace the insights of Jesus. Jesus did not have to call on the sanctions of the law in order to maintain his teachings about the sanctity of marriage. Jesus was not afraid that his forgiving of an adulteress would be a condoning of adultery. On the other hand, in the light of his understanding of righteousness, Jesus knew that even if a society should have such efficient law enforcement that there was one hundred percent obedience to the law, there still might not be a single righteous person in the society. Jesus thus did not believe that upholding an ethical ideal and having a law with sanctions to support the ideal were synonymous. Where Christianity consents to become a civil religion, it always loses the vision of justification. Caught in the paternalistic view that we are to be our brother's keeper, it insists upon laws to enforce the way of life that ought to be the fruit of the gospel. It becomes more concerned that people behave themselves than that they should become righteous in the Biblical sense of the term.

Where a church has grown accustomed to thinking in paternalistic terms in the realm of general morals, it becomes very difficult for it to relate to the problems of minority groups. Where there is racial discrimination it is natural for the dominant race to take a paternalistic "white man's burden" attitude toward the oppressed race. No form of discrimination is more infuriating to the oppressed than the patronizing goodwill of the oppressor who stoops from his superior position to be kind to the lesser breeds without the law. James Cone speaks for the oppressed: "To whites who want to know what they can do (a favorite question of oppressors), Black Theology says: 'Keep your damn mouth closed, and let us black people get our thing together.' " [26] The anger in Cone's words comes from resentment at the implied superiority of the white man who deigns to be of service to those whom he sees as his inferiors.

Where religion sees itself as its brother's keeper, it is almost totally incapable of being of any help to a situation of oppression. Such a religion will inevitably interpret love to the oppressed in terms of keeping inferior beings for their own good. A leader of the Indian and Métis people in western Canada refuses all invitations to speak to church groups. He says that it would be a waste of time because Christians are so "missionary minded" that the only way they can try to help people is to remold the others in their own image. There can be no doubt that often there is a truly good will in the paternalistic person. He or she truly desires to be helpful, but the habits of paternalistic religion are well taught and cannot be laid aside easily.

Central to the doctrine of justification is a willingness to let people be themselves. Knowing that righteousness cannot be imposed from the outside but must arise from within, the believer in justification will be prepared to accept other persons where they are. As the father in Jesus' parable gave his son the freedom to go into the far country, so believers in justification will know that they are not called to impose their views upon others. In a racial situation this will help us to see that the last thing the oppressed person needs is a keeper. That has been his problem from the beginning, he has been kept. Even when his keepers were benevolent, he was not allowed to be a full person in his own right. He needs us to get off his back and that may mean keeping our mouth shut even when we feel that we have pearls of superior wisdom to give him. It means letting him have responsibility for his destiny even though we fear that he is not ready for such responsibility. The paradox of responsibility always is that if it is not given to those who are not ready for it, no one ever will be responsible. We only can become responsible by being given the freedom to be responsible. Here too the gamble has to be taken.

Where religion is filled with a sense of its obligation to provide a sacred canopy for the ideals of the *status quo*, it is almost impossible for it to understand the doctrine of justification. It dares not take the gamble that Jesus took of seeking a righteousness that is not imposed from the outside. Inevitably it sees society in terms of the keepers of the law and those who must be kept in their place. The keepers of the law always feel that they have attained a position from which it is their duty to cast the first stone. But a major thrust of Jesus' teaching was to repudiate the assumption that society can be so neatly divided into the well and the sick, the good and the evil. Even those who felt that they had done all things required by God or man were admonished to count themselves as unworthy servants (Luke 17:10). This leads us to the next theme that must be examined: the place of forgiveness in the doctrine of justification.

IV

The Forgiveness of God

IN THE INTRODUCTION I noted the danger of using the abbreviation "justification by faith alone." In leaving out the reference to grace, the abbreviation tempts us to think of faith as a work that we must perform in order that we be justified before God. Given the tendency of the modern world to identify faith and belief, it is not surprising to find many Protestants who believe that the requirement for salvation is that they believe the doctrines taught by the church. The Reformers were very much concerned about distinguishing their understanding of justification from the idea that one is justified by believing correct doctrine. Calvin summed it up: "For we do not obtain salvation by our promptitude to embrace as truth whatever the Church may have prescribed, or by our transferring to her the province of inquiry and of knowledge." [27] Justification, for the Reformers, was grounded in God's grace poured out upon his people. Only when this is understood can the meaning of faith be seen.

Grace means "goodwill" or "favor" and normally implies that the goodwill and favor are freely given. It often has the implication of goodwill shown by a superior to an inferior. Thus a king might act graciously toward one of his subjects, but it would sound a bit strange to say that the subject acted graciously toward his king. Furthermore, there is usually some implication that a gracious action is one that goes beyond what is earned or deserved.

When the Bible speaks of God's grace it is always rooted in the presupposition of God's love. To say that God is gracious is to say that God loves his children so that his relationship to them is not based simply upon what they deserve from him. When we stand before God we stand as ones who have deserved his ill favor and judgment. But a gracious God does not hold our sins against us. He is ever ready to forgive. Justification by grace begins with the affirmation that our sins are forgiven by God.

Forgiveness: Personal and Legal

Forgiveness becomes relevant in a situation where someone has committed an offense against another. However, we do tend to use the term "forgiveness" to apply to two quite different kinds of situations. In a legal context we tend to feel that the guilty party has put himself into debt to the injured person or to society. Something is thus owed to the injured party or to society, and if restitution cannot be made in any other way, punishment may be inflicted upon the guilty one. In this legal context, forgiveness means generosity on the part of the injured parties, whereby they do not require that the debt be paid. It is important, however, to see that when we use the word "forgiveness" in such a legal context, it is a case of a derived meaning. The term arises from, and properly belongs to, the realm of interpersonal relationships where the key concept is "reconciliation." When an intimate personal relationship of love or friendship has been broken by one of the parties, there is the need of reconciliation. Forgiveness, in this context, means the willingness of the injured party to enter again into the former relationship.

In the legal context the debt or punishment is a central factor. Objectively, the guilty party owes something and the situation can be rectified only if the debt is paid or punishment is inflicted, on the one hand, or by the injured party forgiving and thus waiving the debt or penalty on the other hand. But in interpersonal relations there is nothing to be gained by thinking in terms of punishment or debt. A bystander, looking on objectively, may argue that the guilty party now owes the injured one something. But if true reconciliation is to occur, it is important that the person involved in the broken relationship should not think in those terms. If the injured party insists that the friendship or love relationship cannot be restored until the guilty party has paid, it becomes almost impossible for the relationship to be restored. A criminal can properly speak of having paid his debt to society when he has finished his prison term. But in the delicacy of interpersonal relationships, at what point can the guilty party claim that the debt has been paid in full to the injured one? How many mink coats does an unfaithful husband owe to his wife before he can be said to have paid the debt of his infidelity? The problem in such relations is not *paying* a debt, but in letting bygones be bygones and reentering the relationship that has been broken.

In the legal context forgiveness may be costly. The penalty or debt is waived and those exercising forgiveness have been denied what was coming to them. But it is in the personal realm that we see the really costly nature of forgiveness. It is not a cost that can be measured as in the case of the legal debt that is waived. The injured parties who forgive must bear within themselves all of the hurt, anger, resentment, and pain that comes from the injury that they have received. In a legal situation forgiveness is usually pure joy to the forgiven. Having been found in debt, they hear the good news that they do not have to pay the debt after all. But it is not that easy in personal relationships. In one of his sermons Harry Emerson Fosdick said that whenever he heard someone speak about the joy of being forgiven, he knew that person had never experienced being forgiven. Fosdick obviously was thinking of personal relationships. When we know that we have injured those whom we love and that they have borne the pain and agony of what we have done and nonetheless have restored the relationship, there is joy, yes, but it is a joy deeply mixed with pain.

When we have been forgiven by a loved one, we know that he or she has borne the pain of our action. Thus it is difficult to accept this forgiveness. The guilty party has the humiliation of knowing that he stands before the other in a helpless situation. Christians may blithely sing the old hymn line, "Nothing in my hand I bring," but the real experience is not pleasant. A guilty husband has nothing in his hand to bring to his injured wife, and that is painful. This is why we always try to do something to atone, since it makes us feel a bit better about being forgiven. It is difficult to say whether it is more painful to forgive a real interpersonal injury or to be forgiven for one. But, in the final analysis, the relationship can be restored only when thoughts of payment or waiving payment are transcended and the two persons each accept their pain and hurt and pick up where they left off. As long as either of them insists upon thinking in terms of the payment of a debt or the inflicting of punishment, or even the waiving of it, the relationship will not be the same. The debt will hang between them as a skeleton at every meeting.

In the history of theology God's forgiveness of sinful humanity often has been pictured in a legal context. Humanity, through its sin, owes a debt to God; it is deserving of punishment. As the moral ruler of the universe, God cannot simply waive this debt or punishment, because that would undermine the moral order. Therefore, complicated doctrines of atonement have been worked out to demonstrate that God has not, in fact, waived the debt or punishment. Jesus has paid the debt and he has suffered the punishment. Such doctrines of atonement are usually called "Anselmic," because the classic expression of such doctrines came from the eleventh-century theologian Anselm. It has always been a question whether such doctrines can claim a Biblical foundation. Some Scripture texts can be quoted that seem to support them. But in these cases there remains the question whether such passages are meant to teach a legal view of forgiveness or whether they are analogies. The question cannot be answered by analyzing isolated Biblical passages. We must examine the Biblical message as a whole and decide if the relationship between God and his people is to be understood in legal or in personal terms. It is my thesis that only personal terms can do justice to the message of the Bible in general and to the teachings of Jesus in particular.

In the Bible, forgiveness is set in the context of the personal relationship that God seeks to have with his people. The problem is not a debt and its payment, but it is the task of restoring humanity to that relationship with God which has been lost. Forgiveness and reconciliation are therefore always joined in the Scriptures. Paul does not say that God was in Christ paying humanity's debt or suffering its punishment. Rather he says, "God was in Christ reconciling the world to himself, not counting their trespasses against them" (II Cor. 5:19).

When Jesus centered upon family relationships as the basic analogy for the relationship of God and his people, he set the whole question into the realm of personal relationships. God, for Jesus, is the Father. When his prodigals return, as we have seen, they are not forced to become hired servants in order to pay a debt and thus earn a place again in the home. They are forgiven with joy and restored to the intimacies of the family circle.

This point is confirmed by another of Jesus' parables, that of the laborers in the vineyard (Matt. 20:1–16). In this parable the owner of the vineyard goes out at various hours of the day and hires more men to work his vineyard. When the day is over and the wages are being paid, those who had worked but an hour received the same wage as those who had labored all day. In legal terms this is a baffling parable. Surely it is not good economic sense for the vineyard owner to act this way and, worse still, it is not even just. Why should those who worked through the heat of the day get no more than those who were only there for the cool evening hour? Jesus chose this parable to show that our relationship to God cannot be put within the legal framework. If we think in terms of personal relationships, the point of the parable becomes clear. The good parent does not love the first-born child more than the last-born. Nor does the good parent have more love for the child who has done more for the parent.

The parable of the prodigal son brings this out clearly, for the prodigal and the respectable stay-at-home are equally dear to the father. When the respectable son protests because his brother has been freely forgiven, he has the law on his side. The prodigal is in debt to both the father and the brother and he should not be restored to the home until he has paid. But, as the father gently reminds the elder son, this is a matter of personal family relationships: "This your brother was dead, and is alive" (Luke 15:32). The elder son is reminded that, although from a legal standpoint he may have a good case, this is not a legal matter. This is his brother, his father's son, and the relationship cannot be ruled by legal niceties.

The good news that is in Jesus Christ is summed up well by John 1:17: "For the law was given through Moses; grace and truth came through Jesus Christ." The coming of Jesus reveals that God's relationship to his people is to be seen not in legal terms but in terms of grace and truth. The Father forgives the sins of his children and the parent-child relationship between God and his children is restored. The heavenly Father actively seeks to win his erring children back to him: "While we were yet sinners Christ died for us" (Rom. 5:8). When the sinner repents and the relationship is restored, there is rejoicing in heaven (Luke 15:7).

This is not the time or place to work out a doctrine of atonement. I have been critical of those doctrines which put the atonement into a legal rather than a personal framework. But even in those doctrines, there is a truth. In emphasizing the need of Christ to die to bring about atonement, they have borne witness to the fact that forgiveness is costly. In personal relationships, when the injured parties forgive, they bear in themselves the pain and hurt of what has been done. Theologians have a profound insight when, in their doctrines of atonement, they see in the sufferings of Christ a revelation of the pain God experiences in forgiving his fallen children. Probably no doctrine of atonement can do justice to the depths of mystery that we encounter here, but one thing is clear: God's revelation in Christ means that we can proclaim to all persons that God has forgiven their sins.

Forgiveness and Repentance

But here we find that many Christians become uncomfortable because they cannot really proclaim that God forgives everyone their sins. Surely, they feel, God does not forgive the unrepentant. God is willing to forgive, but even God cannot forgive us if we do not repent. If God forgave the unrepentant, he would be condoning their sin. And so in liturgies and other expressions of Christian faith we have spoken to the effect that "whosoever repents of his sins may be forgiven." This is not an entirely incorrect way to speak, but it does have a danger. It is likely to lead people to feel that repentance is something that they must do in order to obtain, earn, or deserve God's forgiveness. In that case repentance becomes a work necessary for salvation and we are not saved by God's grace alone.

If repentance is a work necessary to achieve God's forgiveness, we are left with the problem that always haunts a doctrine of salvation by works. How much work is necessary? In popular thought, repentance is defined as feeling sorry for our misdeeds. How sorry do we have to feel? To what degree are we really sorry for what we have done and to what degree are we simply sorry about the consequences to us? The child caught stealing cookies is very sorry—sorry that he has been caught and will be punished, but not necessarily sorry that he took the cookies. How can we be sure that we feel the right kind of sorrow for our sins?

In the Bible forgiveness is often linked to repentance, but there is no evidence that repentance is a cause of God's forgiveness. Jesus certainly spoke words of forgiveness where there were no signs of repentance. The best example of this is seen in his words from the cross, "Father, forgive them; for they know not what they do" (Luke 23:34). As we read the context, there is no evidence that Jesus' crucifiers were showing any signs of repentance; on the contrary, they were getting sadistic pleasure from making him suffer and they were greedily casting lots for his clothes. Likewise,

Jesus shocked the Pharisees by proclaiming that the paralytic's sins had been forgiven (Mark 2:5; Matt. 9:2; Luke 5:20). We are not given any reason to think that the paralytic had shown any signs of repentance.

To return again to the parable of the prodigal: Was he forgiven only when he returned home, and was he forgiven because he returned home? Surely not! If someone had known the mind of the father, he could have gone to the son in the far country with the good news: Your father forgives you, why do you not return home? What we are saying is that the father's attitude toward the son was not changed by the son's returning home. The only change that occurred was that the son, by returning home, put himself in a position to experience the father's forgiveness. The two were reconciled.

Luther, in his Large Catechism, commenting upon the petition for forgiveness in the Lord's Prayer, says: "Here again there is great need to call upon God and pray, 'Dear Father, forgive us our debts.' Not that he does not forgive sin even without and before our prayer; and he gave us the Gospel, in which there is nothing but forgiveness, before we prayed or even thought of it. But the point here is for us to recognize and accept this forgiveness." [28] Luther is correct in picturing God's forgiveness, as portrayed in Christ, to be unconditionally given. It does not wait for us to repent or to pray for it.

God seeks a personal relationship with his children. When the relationship is broken by the sin of the children, God freely forgives them. His love for them does not waver, and he refuses to give up on them. He seeks them out where they are. But because God seeks a personal relationship with us, the relationship depends upon our free response to God's forgiving love. The father has forgiven his son even in the far country, but the son cannot be reconciled so long as he stays there. He has to come home and accept his father's forgiveness. As Paul Tillich so aptly phrased it, we must "accept our acceptance."

In the Bible the word "repentance" does not mean primarily remorse or sorrow for sin, it means a turning around, a change of direction; it is the prodigal coming home. Because there is pain involved in accepting forgiveness from a loved one, we can assume that the sinner who turns around and returns to God will feel sorrow and remorse. That is why it is so easy to think of sorrow and remorse first when we hear the word "repent." But a person may have a great deal of sorrow and remorse about who and what he is without ever turning back to God. Despite his wearing sackcloth and ashes, he may not have repented in the Biblical sense.

Where someone has broken a personal relationship, the word that the injured party has forgiven the guilty one can be a very powerful motivation causing the offender to seek reconciliation. Thus there is a causal relationship between repentance and forgiveness, but in God's case it is never our repentance that causes God's forgiveness; rather, it is God's forgiveness that causes our repentance.

However, there is a group of Jesus' sayings which seems to contradict what has been said. In the Lord's Prayer we are taught to pray to be forgiven as we forgive (Matt. 6:12). When Jesus finished teaching this prayer, he commented upon only one part of it, saying, "For if you forgive men their trespasses, your heavenly Father also will forgive you; but if you do not forgive men their trespasses, neither will your Father forgive your trespasses" (Matt. 6:14–15). This seems clearly to say that God's forgiveness is conditional upon our forgiving others. We come across the same theme in the parable of the unmerciful servant (Matt. 18:23–35). A servant had been forgiven a large debt by his king.

However, the servant turned around and had a fellow servant thrown into jail for failure to pay a small debt. Upon hearing of this, the king had the first servant jailed. Jesus closes by saying, "So also my heavenly Father will do to every one of you, if you do not forgive your brother from your heart" (Matt. 18:35). Again, in Mark 11:25, Jesus admonishes his hearers to forgive their neighbors "so that your Father also who is in heaven may forgive you your trespasses."

What are we to make of this set of teachings? Is Jesus prescribing a work which must be performed if we are to be forgiven? If so, then the refusal to forgive becomes an unforgivable sin—at least until such time as we change our attitude. There is a sense in which an unforgiving attitude holds a unique place among sins. If we begin from the premise that all of us have fallen short of what we are called to be and are hence sinners, then the unforgiving person is a moral prig who goes on casting the first stone despite his own sin. Everyone sympathizes with the king in the parable of the unmerciful servant. When the king sees that the man whom he has forgiven of a major debt is unwilling to forgive the small debt of another, it is enough to cause the anger in which the king takes back his forgiveness and treats the unmerciful without mercy. The prodigal son in the parable had no doubt committed scores of sins, but it is easier to forgive all of them than it is to forgive the sin of the elder brother who refused to forgive his brother. It seems appropriate that Jesus closes the parable with the forgiven prodigal celebrating in the father's house while the unforgiving elder brother remains outside sulking. Yet if forgiving others is a work that we must perform to win God's forgiveness, we are back with all the problems of works-righteousness. When have we forgiven enough? Is it enough to have expressed forgiveness of our neighbor, even though bitterness remains in our hearts over what has been done? Will God hold the bitterness against us and refuse to forgive us?

A problem that we have here is that we tend to fall back into thinking of forgiveness in its legal context, where it means the waiving of a penalty or debt. The problem needs to be examined in the light of God's will to enter into the Father-child relationship with his people. To be in that relationship with God is so to love God that his will becomes our will and his ways our ways. It is a primary characteristic of God and his gracious love that he is always willing to forgive. God's forgiveness is offered to us so that no matter what our sin, we are always free to come again into the relationship with him. But how can we be in this relationship with God if our hearts are filled with a desire for revenge upon those whom God also has forgiven? Refusing to forgive is not a crime of such magnitude that it cannot be forgiven; God forgives the unmerciful also. The problem is that so long as we are unmerciful we refuse to enter again into the relationship with God and we are unable to accept our acceptance.

This point is illustrated in Jesus' parable about the prodigal. There is a danger in the popular terminology that refers to Jesus' parable of "the prodigal son," for it is a parable of two sons. Furthermore, if we look to the context in which Jesus told the parable, it would seem that he intended the part about the elder son as the primary point. Luke tells us that he told this and the parables of the lost sheep and the lost coin when the Pharisees and scribes were murmuring because "this man receives sinners and eats with them" (Luke 15:2). Like the Pharisees and scribes, the elder son was a righteous person. He had not gone into the far country to waste his father's inheritance on harlots and wild living but had stayed home and worked as a faithful son. When the prodigal returned and was forgiven and entertained, the elder son was bitter. As human beings we cannot but have some sympathy with the elder brother. We know how he must have felt to see his wayward brother at the center of so much attention and good will. He could not help wondering if it paid to be good. But the point of the parable is that his unforgiving attitude had shut him out of the father's house.

There certainly was forgiveness for the elder brother on the part of the father. We even read that the father "came out and entreated him" when he refused to go into the house (Luke 15:28). The father's action reveals clearly that it is not the father's will to punish the elder son by shutting him out of the house. But the elder son had shut himself out because he could not stand being in the same house where his brother is forgiven. This would seem to be the point in Jesus' statements about forgiveness to those who do not forgive. It is not that God will not forgive the unforgiving but that the unforgiving shut themselves out of the relationship with God by refusing to be reconciled.

One of the problems in understanding Jesus at this point is the individualism of our North American Protestantism. Recently there was a popular song that sang about "Me and Jesus, we've got our own thing going." That song summed up much of what we think about Christianity. Even if most of us would be mindful of good manners and sing of "Jesus and me," we do tend to think of our relationship to God as a one-to-one, lonely kind of affair. When me and Jesus have our own thing going, then I've got it made. But the New Testament presents a radically social view of the God-person relationship. Never does the New Testament speak of "saint" in the singular. To be a saint—that is, to be in the right relationship with God—is to be a member of the community of saints. If it were simply a matter of me and

Jesus, then Jesus' words about forgiving in order that we might be forgiven would end up as a work we had to perform in order to be forgiven. But when we see the social nature of sainthood, Jesus' words take on a different meaning. To be a forgiven saint in God's presence is to be a forgiven and forgiving member of God's people. We cannot have a relationship with God that does not include others. The elder son wanted a relationship with his father that would shut out a relationship with his brother. But that was not possible, because the brother was in the home, and if the elder brother could not stand to be in the prodigal's presence, then he could not come into the father's house.

This analysis of forgiveness sheds further light on why the action of Protestant churches so often belies their teaching about justification. The Pharisees and scribes of Jesus' day were good churchgoing, law-abiding citizens. They shut themselves out of fellowship with Jesus because they could not tolerate or forgive the sinners with whom Jesus mixed so freely. This has remained the temptation of the church in every age. Seeing itself as the upholder of public morality, it has been hesitant to express in action the forgiveness of the sins of others. It is difficult for the average congregation to express real forgiveness to the outcasts of its community until the outcasts reform themselves so that they are worthy of fellowship. Instead of forgiving the prodigals, we prefer to see the prodigals first prove themselves by being faithful hired servants for a time.

Forgiving Sins or Condoning Sins?

The problem is that it is difficult to distinguish between forgiving sins and condoning them. To the Pharisees it seemed that when Jesus mixed so freely with sinners, he was condoning their sin. The church always has had to wrestle with the problem that haunted the Pharisees. But today the problem seems especially difficult because it is popular to describe our times as a permissive age. We are a culture, so it is said, that takes a light view of sins. We say that everyone is doing it and thus it cannot be wrong. In the permissive society the sinner is perfectly acceptable because his sin is condoned. If the church, in such a situation, tries to practice forgiveness, it will simply seem to have capitulated to the permissiveness of society. It will have lost its ability to make an ethical difference in its world. Therefore, before the church can practice forgiveness it must have some signs of repentance and a changed life on the part of the sinner. Only then can the church practice forgiveness without seeming to condone the sin.

At first sight this argument seems persuasive, but we must stop and ask what we mean by a permissive society. In North America it usually refers to the standards that deal with the area of sex. Evidence that we have become a permissive society consists of the easier attitude taken toward premarital sex, the greater freedom from censorship of literature, pictures, or movies that deal with sex, more liberalized laws on abortion, and the greater acceptability of divorce. Sometimes attitudes toward the use of illegal drugs are added to the list of evidence for the permissive society. But before we become too certain that we are a permissive society, it might be well to paraphrase a famous observation and remember: All societies are permissive; they are just permissive about different things. A hundred and fifty years ago North American society was permissive toward slavery. Society as a whole legalized slavery and protected the slave owner's property rights, which included the owning of another human being. Slave owners were respected members of churches, but this was seldom seen as a forgiveness of their sin of owning slaves. Inasmuch as slavery was not seen as a sin there was no need to express forgiveness for it. In the late nineteenth century, North American society was permissive with regard to lying, stealing, cheating, and exploiting people when it was done in the process of becoming a multimillionaire. The robber barons of "the gilded age" were accepted into the church, not as forgiven sinners, but as the cornerstones upon which the churches were built. Seminaries and other church institutions were named after them. Up to the late 1950's North American society was extremely permissive toward the sins of racial discrimination. It is still quite permissive in this realm, although there has been some change and it is more likely today that people will experience some guilt feelings about more flagrant expressions of racial discrimination than was the case in the early 1950's.

Perhaps the Pharisees were not entirely wrong in seeing an element of condoning sin in Jesus' attitude toward the outcast sinners. In mixing with those branded as the notorious sinners of his time, Jesus was proclaiming that their sins did not appear so serious when compared to the sins being condoned by the respectable people. This comes out clearly when Jesus asked why his hearers could see the speck in their brother's eye while never noticing the log in their own. Worse, he notes that they are anxious to take the speck out of their brother's eye but are not even interested in getting the log out of their own (Matt. 7:3–5). Jesus calls this hypocrisy and calls on his respectable audience to clean the logs out of their own eyes so that they can see to take the speck out of the brother's eye. The same theme is seen when Jesus called upon the person who was without sin to cast the first stone at the adulteress. It was implied when Jesus defended the prostitute who loved much because she had been forgiven much as over against the Pharisee who loved little because he had felt little need of forgiveness. If

Jesus' attitude toward the sinners of the time was not a simple condoning of their sins, it was at least a way of saying that these sins, selected by society for condemnation, were neither the only sins nor the worst sins.

In theory, the line between condoning sin and forgiving sin can be drawn quite sharply and clearly. To forgive sin is quite different from condoning it, because the very definition of forgiveness implies a recognition that the forgiven one is guilty of something. On the other hand, to condone something means, by definition, that we overlook any guilt that may be involved. But while the difference between forgiveness and condoning is easy to define, it is very difficult to express in practice.

We can find guidance on how to walk the narrow line between forgiveness and condoning in the practice of Jesus. It is noteworthy that whereas Jesus was the friend of the outcast sinners, he spoke ringing words of judgment against the religious leaders. For example, the twenty-third chapter of Matthew is a series of harsh judgments upon the Pharisees and scribes, with special concern about their hypocrisy. Scholars have had difficulty with such passages. To some it has seemed that Jesus' treatment of the religious leaders fell below his own teaching about forgiving sins, since Jesus does not sound very forgiving in this chapter. Others have argued that such passages were the creation of the church and expressed the church's later conflict with the religious leaders. Thus Sherman Johnson, in his exegesis of Matt., ch. 23, for *The Interpreter's Bible*, suggests that the Gospels have exaggerated Jesus' denunciation of the Pharisees.

It would seem likely that Matthew did exercise some editorial privileges in bringing together into a lengthy discourse a series of condemnations of the Pharisees. Nonetheless, it is clear that Jesus was harsh toward the religious leadership. We know that the religious leaders continually tried to capture him in compromising statements that could be used against him, and finally they played a major role in bringing about his crucifixion. It would be difficult to explain such attitudes if Jesus had had nothing to say against the religious leaders. Furthermore, it is important to remember that Jesus' criticism of the religious leaders did not mean that he was unprepared to forgive them. He visited in their homes when he had the opportunity, he gave serious answers to their serious questions, and his words of forgiveness from the cross no doubt include all who were responsible for bringing him there.

There was consistency in Jesus' attitudes toward the outcast sinners on the one hand and toward the Pharisees and scribes on the other hand. When Jesus came to the outcasts, he moved among a group that was branded as sinful by public consensus. These outcasts had no illusions about where they stood in the public eye. To such ones Jesus had no words of condemnation because the last thing that they needed was another voice to tell them what loathsome sinners they were. To them Jesus brought the good news that they were loved and forgiven by God. But the Pharisees had a different problem. Being on the whole a good and righteous group, they had no idea that they too were sinners in need of forgiveness. They needed no pat on the back for their virtues because they were busy patting their own backs (Luke 18:11). What they needed was to have their complacency punctured so that they could come to see themselves as fellow sinners with those whom they condemned. Words of forgiveness would not be meaningful to the Pharisees until they had first come to see that there was a need to be forgiven. Pascal said that there were only two groups of people in the world—the righteous who know that they are sinners and the sinners who believe that they are righteous. That may be somewhat of an oversimplification, but it seems to be in basic harmony with Jesus' practice. Because they knew that they were sinners, the outcasts of Jesus' time had taken the first step toward righteousness, while the religious leaders, believing themselves to be righteous, were blind to their problem. Those who know that they are sinners need the hope that comes from learning that the past is forgiven so that the future can be different. Those who think of themselves as righteous, however, need the harsh word of the law that reveals them to be sinners before they too can hear the good news that they are forgiven. To express forgiveness to them at an earlier stage would be to condone their sin.

Jesus' attitudes toward these two groups can also be understood in terms of the relationship of each group to the law. Those who were branded as sinners in Jesus' time were people who had failed to live up to the demands of the religious law. They knew that they were incapable of making themselves righteous by obeying the demands of the law. So, in most cases, they no longer made any effort to keep the law's many requirements. Compared to these sinners, the religious leaders had done a good job of keeping the law; hence they were scrupulous in trying to make themselves righteous by obeying the law. To those who had given up on keeping the law, Jesus spoke the good news that they would not be judged by the law; that they were in the hands of a gracious and forgiving Father. But to those who still put themselves under the law, Jesus brought the message that they who lived under the law would be judged by the law. So long as one chooses to live under the law, however, it is not enough to be comparatively better than someone else. As James put it, "For whoever keeps the whole law but fails in one point has become guilty of all of it" (James 2:10). And thus all who would live by the law are condemned by the law.

All too often the church's practice has been the opposite of the pattern found in Jesus. Seeing itself as the protector of the public morality, it has joined the general hue and cry against those who are publicly condemned as sinners, while it has left undisturbed the sins of the complacent, respectable people. The church calls for strict enforcement of laws against prostitutes but has been slow to back laws that would protect racial minorities from the discrimination practiced by "respectable" society. Churches have been much more enthusiastic about condemning the illegal use of drugs than they have been about challenging the way in which the respectable middle class has built a drug culture through the use of legal drugs. All too often Christians have been more ready to condemn the practice of abortion than they have been to point out the sins of a society that allows so many of its children to be blighted by life in the slums.

The tendency of the churches to condemn deviation from the social norms has resulted in a considerable alienation of youth in recent years. Young people have been made to feel uncomfortable in the churches because they were continually condemned for any behavior that departed from the social norm. For example, a few years ago many sermons were preached to criticize the length of hair worn by young people. No doubt many of the older generation have been alienated by the churches' criticism of nonconformity, but they have left the church quietly. The younger generation has been more vocal in their criticism of the churches. Their criticism helps us to see that wherever such attitudes have been present the practice of the churches says that those are justified who keep their noses clean and live a good, respectable life. In the light of this practice, the preaching of justification loses its credibility.

When all has been said, there can be no question that the preaching of forgiveness always runs the risk of seeming to condone sin. Always there will be some who, hearing the good news of God's graciousness, will decide to sin so that grace may be more abundant (Rom. 6:1; cf. 3:8). Luther recognized that his preaching was leading to this result. Does this mean, he asked, that we should quit preaching forgiveness because of the abuse? His answer was a ringing "no." Taking comfort from the fact that Jesus and Paul had been similarly misunderstood, he concludes with a typically pungent statement. "Nor should we pay attention to how our doctrine is abused by the vicious and wicked rabble, who cannot be cured whether they have the Law or not. On the contrary, we should pay attention to how suffering consciences are to be counseled, lest they perish with the wicked rabble." [29] Luther here is in harmony with the practice of Jesus. Despite the danger that some will use the teaching of forgiveness to condone sin, forgiveness must be offered to all who suffer the pangs of guilt or who stand condemned by society. The words of condemnation and judgment are to be reserved for those who feel no need of being forgiven because they find nothing wrong with themselves.

V

Liberation from Sin

Sin and Sins

When the word "sin" is spoken in our culture, it brings to the minds of most people a list of forbidden actions or deeds. It is a sin to lie or cheat or steal or to commit adultery or to commit murder. Different people will have different lists of sins. Some will go on to include such things as drinking alcoholic beverages, smoking, and going to the movies, abortion, birth control, and divorce. Some have even included the drinking of coffee. But whatever the list of sins we may have, it is generally agreed that people are free moral beings who have to decide whether or not they will commit specific sins. Day in and day out, people make decisions to do good or evil. No one may be perfect, but some people do a pretty good job of deciding; they perform more good deeds than sins and hence are seen as the righteous. Within religious circles they are seen as the ones who are pleasing to God. But other people commit sins more frequently than they perform good deeds, and they are thus the sinners who are properly condemned by God and man.

Because of the tendency to view religion as the guardian of public morality, and because of the popular notion of sin

as forbidden actions, there are those who think that the
social purpose of religion is to motivate people so that they
will be more likely to do good deeds and less likely to
commit sins. When people think this way they find the
doctrine of justification baffling. How can we motivate
people to do the good and not commit sins when we keep
preaching that our good deeds do not make us righteous
before God and that our sins can readily be forgiven? It is
not surprising that the doctrine has been widely held to be
the death of ethics or of concern with living a Christian life.
At the time of the Reformation the Anabaptist groups were
shocked at the lack of reformed life in the churches of
Luther and Calvin. No doubt there was reason for their
being shocked. Luther himself was grieved at how some
were using his preaching as a rationalization for doing
nothing about living their faith. On one occasion, having
noted that some of his followers were using his doctrine to
justify themselves for not helping the poor or overcoming
their own vices, he says, "The grief hereof maketh me
sometimes so impatient, that many times I wish such swine
which tread precious pearls under their feet, were yet still
remaining under the tyranny of the Pope." [30]

So long as the popular view of sin is held, the doctrine of
justification can only lead to what Dietrich Bonhoeffer
called "cheap grace." Cheap grace, says Bonhoeffer,
"means the justification of sin without the justification of the
sinner. Grace alone does everything, they say, and so
everything can remain as it was before." [31] Since sin means
freely choosing the wrong action and since justification
assures me of acceptance by God in spite of what I choose,
why bother to make difficult choices or try to improve my
life? Why not follow the line of least resistance and remain
as I am, assured that my sins are forgiven? Certainly I do

not need to worry about the hard sayings of Jesus about loving my neighbor as myself.

The Bible, however, gives a different picture of sin. Sin is not a matter of freely choosing to do the wrong action instead of the right one; it is a fatal sickness. Jesus compared sin with sickness when he said that it is not the well but the sick who need a physician (Mark 2:17). In Eph. 2:1 people are described as being dead in trespasses and sins, and such a death is contrasted with a new life in Christ. Paul describes baptism as a dying of the old self and a rising to a new life in Christ (Rom. 6:4). In John 3:3, Jesus tells Nicodemus that unless a person is "born anew" he cannot see the Kingdom of God. The language here implies something more drastic than the making of resolutions or deciding to act better in the future.

The best way to summarize the Biblical view of sin is to see it as bondage. This is brought out vividly in a dialogue between Jesus and his fellow Jews. Jesus tells his hearers that the truth will make them free (John 8:32). The Jews object that, being sons of Abraham, they have never been in bondage to anyone. Jesus replies, "Truly, truly, I say to you, every one who commits sin is a slave to sin" (John 8:34). Sin as bondage was a central theme of the Reformation and was emphasized by both Luther and Calvin. It is no accident that this passage from John is the assigned reading for Reformation Day in the Lutheran churches.

Sin as bondage makes no sense to those who hold the popular view of sin. Where sin is seen as a matter of freely choosing to do an evil deed, it would be a contradiction to speak of sin as bondage. Immanuel Kant summed it up succinctly when he said: "If I ought, I can." That is, to say that I ought to do something is to imply logically that I am able to do it. Anytime that I can prove that my action was under compulsion or that some obligation was beyond my capabilities, I am removed from all responsibility. If I cannot swim, there is no sense in saying that I ought to jump into twenty feet of water to save a drowning man. I do not sin when I helplessly watch him drown.

The laws of the land and philosophical discussions of ethics and morals always presuppose that "ought" implies that one can do what is one's duty. In a court of law, if the defendant can be proven to have been criminally insane, he is not punished, because this implies that he was not free when he committed the crime. Ethical and moral theorists almost universally follow Kant's theme which sees that "ought" logically implies the possibility of the agent performing the action. It would be a mistake to place the Biblical view in opposition to legal or philosophical views. A serious confusion arises when we fail to see that the term "sin" is being used with two quite different meanings and for different purposes. The popular view may be called "moralistic." In moralistic conversation, it is quite correct to assume that it is inappropriate to pass judgment upon any person who acts without freedom to do otherwise. In many realms of our life, such as in legal affairs, the moralistic way of speaking is entirely appropriate and adequate. When, however, we speak of sin as bondage, we are not speaking moralistically, we are speaking theologically and are thus concerned with the relationship between God and his people.

There is value in the practice sometimes followed by theologians whereby they distinguish between sin and sins. When the word is used generically in the singular it describes the condition of the person who is in bondage. A symptom of sin is that a person commits sins. In the eyes of the law or of the ethical theorist, the sins are freely chosen and a person is responsible for them. But theologically speaking, we need to look past the sins to the underlying sin, the sickness that needs to be cured, the bondage from which the sinner needs to be set free. This practice of using the terms "sin" and "sins" indicates that the different disciplines are looking at different aspects of the situation, but the fact that the same word is used in both reminds us that there is an intimate relationship between the themes. A theologian who analyzes the bondage of sin is by no means unconcerned with legal, ethical, and moral questions. Justification by grace alone through faith alone ought to produce results in human behavior.

The Freedom of the Will and Bondage

The question of human freedom, usually called the "freedom of the will," has been long debated in philosophy and other disciplines as well as in theology. Somehow the debates never seem to establish any final conclusions. One reason for this failure to arrive at generally acceptable conclusions is that we have so much difficulty in agreeing upon what we mean by "freedom" or "bondage." For example, some modern philosophers have tried to demonstrate simply and clearly that there is freedom of the will by pointing to certain paradigm cases where everyone would agree that we have examples of actions that are freely performed. One such paradigm is that of a happy bridegroom being wed. No father-in-law is in the background with a shotgun; no pressures are being put upon him. He is obviously doing what he wants to do. Ernest Gellner, criticizing this argument, calls it "the Argument from Smiling Bridegrooms." [32]

At first sight it would appear that an uncoerced and happy bridegroom does provide us with a clear example of someone performing a free action, and that thus it is proven that people do have free will. When we say that someone is doing something with a free will, we have in mind someone who does what he wants and is happy to do. In the ordinary use of language we use the term "free" to describe actions that are performed without any external compulsions. Of course, given the ordinary use of language, we often face complicated situations. Did Adolf Eichmann, for example, act freely in committing his atrocities, or was he justified in his defense that he was simply following the orders of his superiors? No doubt a refusal to obey the orders would have brought serious reprisals upon Eichmann. Was that enough to rob him of his freedom to act in the situation so that he was not responsible for what he did? Such a situation raises a number of debatable issues. By and large, however, it would seem that the popular meaning of freedom can be applied to a considerable number of actions in human life. It would seem that we have demonstrated that human beings do have freedom of the will and that whenever they act in this freedom they are morally responsible for their deeds.

But many philosophers are not satisfied. True enough, our bridegroom is happy and he is not physically coerced, but is that enough to define the action as free? What if, having examined the man's childhood and social conditioning, we find that he has been so molded and conditioned that his choosing of this woman was inevitable? Would we still say that he is acting freely? At the very least his happy marriage is the result of his training in a society that holds up marriage as the great romantic culmination of adulthood. What has this done to his freedom? In raising such questions it is obvious that philosophers are struggling to arrive at an acceptable definition of what we mean by freedom of the will or free acts.

Whatever we may conclude about environmental conditioning, a definition of freedom in terms of the lack of external coercion fails completely to deal with what pyschologists call "compulsive behavior." Alcoholics or drug addicts are not acting freely when they drink alcohol or take drugs. Compulsive eaters are not acting freely when they overeat. In these cases the behavior is not coerced by outside pressures, but the persons involved are not free to refrain from their actions. Sometimes it is said that the addict is no longer free but that he was free when he took his first drink or "fix." After all, in our culture there has been plenty of warning about addiction, so the addict is responsible for his present situation even though he is no longer free. But what about the food addict? The popularity of weight-control groups today points up the fact that one of the most dangerous addictions in our society is the addiction to overeating. Responsible authorities inform us that obesity is the most serious health problem in North America and that it is probably the number one underlying cause of death. Yet a great many people find it impossible, on their own efforts, to refrain from overeating. When they look at their overweight condition they feel anxious in view of the statistics on heart attacks, high blood pressure, diabetes, and the rest. When they realize that they are not as good-looking as they ought to be they feel insecure. When they are scolded for their eating habits they feel guilty. But what do compulsive eaters do when they feel anxious, insecure, or guilty? Inevitably they eat. Here is a bondage that cannot be passed off by saying that they were free when they took their first bite of food. Everyone has to eat.

One of the tragedies of human life is that addicts of food, drugs, or alcohol are frequently told that if they just had "willpower," they could solve their problems. But that is simply to say to such people that if they had no problem, they would have no problem—a not very helpful piece of information. Help for such people can only come when groups such as Alcoholics Anonymous or weight-control groups provide the "grace" of an outside power and a supportive community. For such people, freedom comes not as a removal of an outside coercion but as a release from an inner slavery. It is a release that those who have not had the problem can never understand.

In this discussion of free will we have found that the term "freedom of the will" is not easy to define. When freedom of the will is discussed, the debaters often have different definitions of free will. Consequently, what one party to the debate is affirming is not what the other party is denying. Furthermore, a definition that is completely satisfactory for the purposes of one context may be quite inadequate in another context. This is evident when psychiatrists are called to give evidence in criminal cases. The law has certain simple definitions of when actions are free and when not. The adult who is not under external compulsion and who is not "criminally insane" is a free agent and responsible for his actions. But the psychiatrist may see some such people as having had no real choice because, given their psychological history, they were predetermined in their actions. Although not "criminally insane," they were mentally ill and hence not responsible for what they did.

It is not our task to try to reconcile the legal and psychiatric definitions of free and hence responsible action. But since these disciplines operate with different concepts of a free will, it follows that theology may have still other meanings of the freedom of the will.

When one turns to the discussion of free will and bondage in the writings of Luther and Calvin, it is obvious that both recognized that people do have the "Smiling Bridegroom" form of freedom. Both saw that people do as they wish on certain occasions without external compulsion.

In this sense, people do act freely, but both Reformers
objected to calling this "free will." As Calvin put it, "What
end could it answer to decorate a thing so diminutive with a
title so superb?" [33] Luther and Calvin agreed that the term
"freedom of the will" could be properly applied only to
God. Luther summed it up: "It follows now that free
choice is plainly a divine term, and can be properly applied
to none but the Divine Majesty alone; for he alone can do
and does . . . whatever he pleases in heaven and on
earth." [34] This brings out clearly how the Reformers
believed that the primary question was one of power, not of
freedom. No will can be called free if it does not have the
power to achieve what it wishes.

The Reformers' concern with power as the heart of
freedom brings to mind the popular term "willpower." We
have already mentioned the rather heartless way in which
various addicts are told that if they but had willpower, they
could "kick their habit." This is heartless inasmuch as it is
usually said with the implication that if the addict would
pull up his socks as the speaker has done, he could
overcome his plight. But if we leave out the usual
moralizing in the use of the phrase "willpower," it is a
rather useful way of describing what is involved. If the
addict had willpower, the problem could be solved, but
power is precisely what he lacks. What is called compulsive
behavior is human behavior and, in that sense, voluntary
behavior. When people act compulsively they are not being
controlled as a machine is controlled; they are not acting
under the threat of a gun pointed at their head. Furthermore, in some sense they are doing what they want to do.
The alcoholic wants that drink and the food addict wants
that extra piece of cake and so, by many definitions of the
term, they are acting with free will. But they lack power,
and thus their act is compulsive. Even as they do what they

want to do at this moment they know that they are going to
hate themselves tomorrow, but that knowledge is without
power to change their action today.

We noted that the Bible speaks of sin as a sickness and as
bondage. What is implied in such analogies is that humanity does not have within itself the power to achieve that for
which it was created. According to the Scripture, human
beings were created that they might live in the relationship
of love with both God and their neighbor. As Jesus said, the
Law and the Prophets are summed up in the twin commandments to love God with all our heart and mind and
soul and strength and to love our neighbor as ourself. But,
as Reinhold Niebuhr was fond of pointing out, the commandment to love is a paradox, because love cannot be
commanded; it must flow freely and spontaneously. It is
useless to try and exert our willpower to make ourselves
love. By an effort of will we can make ourselves perform
certain good deeds, but we cannot make ourselves do them
for the right motive. And so Paul could say, "If I give away
all I have, and if I deliver my body to be burned, but have
not love, I gain nothing" (I Cor. 13:3).

The Biblical view of righteousness is not a behavioristic
view that looks simply at the outward action. It always
looks within to the motivation of the act. Ultimately people
are called to act with the motivation of love. As Luther and
Calvin analyzed the human condition they were convinced
that we are not free to love, because we do not have the
power to make ourselves love. The medieval church had
lost sight of Paul's point about giving and love. It could
teach that the reason to give alms to the poor was not that
the poor were hungry and starving but in order that the
giver might win salvation for his soul. Such giving is
obviously not motivated by love for the other. Over against
this medieval view (which lives on long after the Middle

Ages) Luther admonished Christians to "Make your gifts freely and for no consideration, so that others may profit by them and fare well because of you and your goodness." [35]

When Luther and Calvin spoke of the bondage of the will they were not denying that people can, within certain limits, do what they want to do. What they were affirming was that people are unable to change their own motivations. They described this bondage vividly by saying that we are "curved in upon ourselves." Created to be curved outward in love to God and neighbor, we find ourselves instead curved in upon ourselves, preoccupied with our own ends. We may give generously to the poor, but we do so in order that we can make ourselves righteous and thereby win favor with God and man. Mankind, curved in upon itself, is capable of a religious concern with God, but it is a concern that inevitably seeks what is in it for the self. The self-centered are religious insofar as they believe that religion is good for them. They are ready to serve God because they believe that such service will win them joy in heaven, protect them from earthly ills, and bring them happiness and peace of mind in this life.

Luther and Calvin emphasized that truly good works could only be performed by the good person. Good works cannot serve to make the performer of them good. A man curved in on himself might do many good deeds, but he would be doing them for the wrong reason. Dietrich Bonhoeffer put the point in a radical way when he said, "It is worse for a liar to tell the truth than for a lover of truth to lie." [36] Bonhoeffer's point brings out the Reformers' position. When the liar tells the truth he performs an act that is good, but the good action cannot make the speaker a good man. When a liar tells the truth we can be sure that it is because this truth serves his ulterior purposes. On the other hand, if a lover of truth tells a lie, there is likely to be a good reason for it.

When sin is seen as a condition of the person rather than the doing of evil actions, it becomes apparent, as Augustine once said, that sin "can take on a high gloss." Jesus pictured this for us vividly in his parable of the Pharisee in the Temple with the publican (Luke 18:9–14). The Pharisee would be welcomed in most neighborhoods as a very fine addition to the community. We would not need to fear that he would steal our money or our wives. We would welcome him into our churches, because—how many tithers do we have? Yet, despite these many good deeds, the man remained a sinner. He was totally curved in upon himself, as was revealed by his prayer thanking God that he was not like other men and by his continual use of first-person pronouns even as he tried to pray to God.

If human bondage consists of being curved in upon oneself, it is obvious that a person would be unable to free himself from his bonds. Anything that the person might do to free himself would recenter his attention upon himself. Self-made persons or those who have overcome undesirable habits are all too likely to end up more centered upon themselves than they were before. They take great satisfaction in what they have accomplished and almost inevitably take a judgmental attitude toward those who have failed to match up with their accomplishments.

One solution to the problem *seems* obvious. If we are too curved in upon ourselves, then we must deny ourselves. The history of religion in general and of Christianity in particular is filled with examples of people who have made radical attempts at self-denial. From the hermits who went into the wilderness to live on pillars, to monastics who whipped themselves, to Puritans who ruthlessly denied

themselves all pleasures, to the modern Protestant who
decides to give until it hurts, there is a long line of persons
who heroically have tried to overcome their self-centeredness by a ruthless denial of the self. But the end product of
self-denial is that inevitably people are more curved in upon
themselves than before. You have to pay a great deal of
attention to yourself if you are going to deny yourself. C. S.
Lewis, in *The Screwtape Letters*, brings this out when he has
the devils substitute the word "unselfishness" for "love."
This, notes Screwtape, encourages a man to surrender
benefits, not so that others will be happy in having them,
but so that he may be unselfish in giving them up.

The law, defined as the laying down of rules with
punishments and rewards attached, is helpless against the
bondage of a person curved in on himself. If such persons
are told that they will go to hell if they do not repent, it may
frighten them. When they are frightened they think more
of themselves and become even more curved in upon
themselves. If they are told of the rewards of heaven, they
get an avaricious gleam in their eyes. The same principle
applies if in place of heaven and hell one substitutes more
worldly punishments and rewards. If it is pointed out that
the self-centered person is never happy, this immediately
motivates such a person to be less self-centered in order that
he may be more happy. He may even go around doing
things for others in order that he may experience the
happiness promised to those who love others.

Luther and Calvin were firmly convinced that the law
could not solve the problem of people in bondage. The only
contribution of the law to salvation, they taught, was that it
might be the means of bringing people to the point of
despairing of their own abilities so that they would throw
themselves upon the grace of God. But by itself the law
could not accomplish even this. A person driven to despair

is just as apt to give up, or to commit suicide, as to repent. The proclamation of the law must be accompanied by the preaching of the gospel.

One of the fascinating things about modern Protestantism is how, in practice, it seems to have forgotten this central understanding of the Reformation. As one listens to the sermons from Protestant pulpits, it becomes clear that the law has replaced the gospel as the central theme. People who go to church have learned to expect that they will be castigated for their sins and that a better way of life will be prescribed to them. They are not often disappointed in these expectations. Churches are identified as places where moral ideals are extolled and people are urged to live up to them. With the law so central in so much Protestant preaching, it is not surprising that the Protestant laity have come to believe in salvation by works.

If being curved in on ourselves cannot be cured by our own efforts, by self-denial, or by the law, how can it be cured? The cure for being curved in upon oneself lies not in denying or hating oneself but in forgetting oneself. Forgetting oneself is, of course, something that we cannot do by our own efforts. The more we concentrate upon forgetting ourselves, the more we think of ourselves. We forget something, not by trying to forget, but by becoming preoccupied with something or someone else. This occurs when we truly love another person. We find that we forget our own interests and seek to satisfy the interests of the loved one. Love is the opposite of being curved in upon oneself. But that brings us back to where we began. Love cannot be commanded, but must arise spontaneously from the heart. The worst form of legalism or preaching of the law is that form which tells us that all we have to do is love. One of the great ironies of the modern world has been the existence of those forms of Christianity which claim they have discovered Christianity to be something simple. They assure us that we do not need to worry about all those dogmas and theologies which are so difficult to believe; all we have to do is love God and our neighbors. Could anything be more simple? Could anything be more intolerably hopeless? How do I make myself loving?

The approach of the gospel is radically different. It begins not by making a demand upon us but by simply affirming, "God loves you." "While we were yet sinners, Christ died for us." What we could not do for ourselves has been done for us; we are forgiven, accepted. The gospel that comes to us in Jesus is the good news that God has acted to come into the far country to live among the pigs with his prodigals. In the gospel there is thus no demand but simply the good news that God's love is with us and for us. The law, with its threats and promises, is forgotten. As John puts it: "There is no fear in love, but perfect love casts out fear. For fear has to do with punishment, and he who fears is not perfected in love" (I John 4:18).

Even in purely human relationships it is obvious that love pulls a person out of the curved-in-upon-oneself syndrome. When a person falls in love with another he begins to think of more than his own pleasures or desires; he becomes concerned to make the other happy. However, such a human relationship may tend to widen the circle of self-interest rather than to free a person from it. Thus a man is drawn from his self-centeredness by his love for his family. Instead of thinking only of himself he thinks of what can make them happy. But such a man may be so centered upon *his* family that he has little time or thought for the needs of anyone else. Similarly, a man's love of his country can lead him to make great sacrifices, even to giving his life, but it is *his* country for which he sacrifices. Love of one's country leads very easily to an idolatrous nationalism that

makes us feel justified in supporting our country in anything
that it does in the national interest.

The love of God pulls a person out of self-centeredness in
a way that is analogous to the way in which love of family or
nation pulls one out of self-centeredness. But love of God is
not limited to one family or nation. Insofar as God's love
claims a person, that person is pulled out of self-centeredness and given a vision of the needs of all persons.

God's grace is God's love in action. We might very well
call our doctrine justification by love through faith. The
love of God revealed in Jesus Christ is a forgiving and
gracious love. It is not directed to the deserving but to the
undeserving. As the father continues to love and forgive the
prodigal in the far country, so God continues to love us
regardless of our merits or demerits. To the one who is
curved in upon himself, God's love comes as a power to pull
him out of himself. John sums it up in beautiful simplicity:
"We love, because he first loved us" (I John 4:19).

The sinner is curved in upon himself and in bondage. He
cannot escape by his own efforts, and threats or promises
only fan his inordinate concern with his own self-interest.
But a free love that comes without conditions attached, a
love that gives itself completely, a love such as we see in
Christ's cross, has the power to free people from the vicious
circle of curved-in-upon-oneself existence.

An old cliché says that religion cannot be taught, it has to
be caught. This cliché takes on a real truth in the present
context. If Christianity is a gracious love that pulls a person
out of the bondage to self, then there are limits to teaching.
Christianity is based upon a Biblical record, historical
events, and certain doctrines, and these can be taught. But
in and of themselves they lack power. People are seldom
won to Christian faith by tracts that are handed to them or
by strangers who come to their door to convert them.

Christian faith is caught when, in the depths of interpersonal relationships, loving concern is manifested.

This raises a serious problem for Christians. They hesitate to point to themselves as examples to be followed, because they are keenly aware that they are still sinners, that they have not attained moral perfection, and therefore that each of them must continually seek God's forgiveness. To some degree, all Christians fail to practice what they preach. But that is not really the point. Witness to others does not lie in moral perfection or in the excellence of lives; it lies in loving concern for the other. A person will be attracted to Christian faith when he finds that a Christian is concerned about him, is ready to share his burdens, and accepts him as he is.

All of this is illustrated by the Christian pastor who may be a poor preacher, a poor administrator, and a poor teacher, but who nonetheless has been with his people in their hours of need. In such a pastor the people recognize a Christian witness that enables them to overlook the obvious deficiencies. Wherever I have been, in the United States and Canada, I have found that church people complain that their pastor does not visit them. I know that pastors have many reasons for this, and that there are many urgent claims upon their time. But perhaps the people have a legitimate complaint. Can a pastor bring the gospel home to his people if he has not taken the time to develop real interpersonal relations with them? If the pastor has not taken the time to sit with them and get to know them, will they feel that depth of concern for them as persons which is called for by the gospel?

If the gospel comes to life in the loving concern of Christians for others, then the failure of the churches to be concerned with liberating the oppressed peoples of the world is a serious witness against the gospel. What does it mean when white North Americans preach about God's seeking love for all, but continue to support the racist society that oppresses racial minorities? How can the poor and the oppressed of the earth be impressed with our preaching when our practice fails to incarnate loving concern? James Cone, in a passage criticizing the white American churches for failing to relate Christianity to the racist society, says: "The white church has not merely failed to render services to the poor, but has failed miserably in being a visible manifestation to the world of God's intention for humanity and in proclaiming the gospel to the world. It seems that the white church is not God's redemptive agent but, rather, an agent of the old society." [37] Cone quite correctly sees that, in failing to fight for the liberation of the oppressed, the churches have failed to preach the gospel. In a later chapter I shall deal more fully with the relationship between the individual and social implications of Christian faith. At this point, however, it is clear that the gospel of God's love ought to stir Christians to see that they are called to express God's love in opposition to all those forces which enslave and degrade God's children.

I have suggested that we might speak of justification by love where we normally speak of justification by grace. We also need to take another look at the term "faith." In the modern world, having faith has come to mean believing something. This connotation of belief is so strong that it is almost impossible for us to understand either the Bible or the Reformation when they speak of justification through faith. Far too many Protestants get the idea that they are saved by believing something. In that case, belief becomes a work that must be performed. Believing the right things is what will justify us. Inevitably, where this view is held, it begins to appear that the more unbelievable something is, the greater the merit for believing it. Protestants thus

proudly proclaim that they are prepared to believe any
absurdity that God asks them to believe and thereby to
demonstrate that their righteous works are greater than the
works of skeptics who have trouble with some of their
doctrines. Furthermore, such Protestants are tempted to set
up rather rigid doctrinal lines to separate themselves from
other Christians who have different theologies. The causes
of the numerous divisions among Protestants are many, but
an important one has been the tendency to see salvation as
dependent upon correct belief. Where that is the case,
theological differences take on eternal consequences. Eternal salvation depends upon the preservation of the purity of
doctrine.

Where Protestantism identifies justification through faith
with justification through belief, it is a strange relapse into
the medieval practices against which the Reformers re-
volted. The medieval church used the Latin term *credentia*
for faith. *Credentia* meant primarily "belief," but it also
implied belief in doctrines or affirmations that were accepted upon some authority. A church, possessed of an
infallible revelation, pronounced the truth, and it was the
duty of the laity to believe submissively what it had been
told. Both Luther and Calvin protested against the view
that the church or its tradition had an unquestionable
authority that must be accepted on pain of damnation. The
essence of the Reformation was the repudiation of the
church's authority. In place of the church's authority
Luther and Calvin placed the authority of God's Word in
Scripture. But even here the faith which they sought was
not *credentia*. The Reformers distinguished a "historical"
belief in the truth of Scripture and a saving faith. It was not
enough to believe that the Scripture was true; after all, even
the devils did that, but they were not saved.

When the Reformers spoke of faith they spoke of *fiducia*,

which means primarily "trust." *Credentia* tends to be an impersonal belief, the authority speaks and we submit our minds and reason to it. But *fiducia*, "trust," is a term that applies properly only within a personal context. If we speak of trusting a thing, the term is used in a derivative and somewhat incorrect sense. Basically, trust is something we have in another person. To trust God is to be in a personal relationship with God; it is to take him at his word. But trust is always closely linked to love. Seldom do we really trust someone unless we love that person. To trust someone is, of course, to believe something about the one trusted, so belief is not absent. But trust goes well beyond simply believing. It involves committing oneself to the other, being willing to put ourselves in his hands.

When, therefore, the Reformers spoke of justification through faith, they meant a justification through trusting God, and we trust God because his love has awakened a loving trust in us. When John says that we love God because he first loved us, he was saying in different words what the Reformers said when they declared that we are saved by grace through faith. In some ways, given the changed meaning of words over the years, John's statement is preferable today because it is less open to misunderstanding.

If we accept God's love with a loving trust, inevitably we desire to please God, because it is of the very nature of love that it wishes to please the loved one. And here is true freedom from bondage. When the law commands us to do certain things under the penalty of punishment for failure to comply, or with the hope of reward if we obey, we are still under bondage. The fear of punishment and the hope of reward restrict us, so that we cannot do what we truly desire to do. But where we act because of love we can act willingly, gladly, and freely. Luther links faith and love with freedom when he says, "Therefore, unless faith gives the light and love makes us free, no man can either have or do anything good, but only evil, even when he performs the good." [38]

No doubt Jesus had in mind this freedom in actions performed out of love when he said that his burden was light (Matt. 11:30). At first sight this statement of Jesus sounds incredible, because the way of life to which he called his disciples was far more rigorous than that required by the Pharisees of his time. "What more are you doing than others?" he asked his disciples (Matt. 5:47). He called his followers to be perfect as God is perfect (Matt. 5:48), and he set an ideal of love that goes far beyond anything envisioned by pharisaical religion. But the point is that the pharisaical religion of his time laid its duties upon people with all of the rewards and penalties of the law attached. Jesus called his disciples into a personal, loving relationship with himself in which they would joyously do his will. It is a well-known aspect of human psychology that hard work never seems hard if we are doing it because we want to do it and not because we have to do it.

It was never the intention of Jesus or the Reformers that Christians should be do-nothing people who rest secure in the belief that their sins are forgiven and who continue to sin "that grace may abound." Rather, it was their intention to free people for an entirely new kind of righteousness, a righteousness that is not a behavioristic obedience to law, rules, or regulations. It is a righteousness that flows gladly and freely from the heart, a spontaneous reaction of love to love. This being so, it is necessary now to turn to examine the life the Christian is called to live in the light of the fact that he is justified by grace alone through faith alone.

VI

The New Life in Christ

Justification and Sanctification

Justification means that the love of God awakens an answering love in the heart of the Christian, and where God is loved there will be the desire to do that which pleases God. To the doctrine of justification, therefore, the Reformers linked the doctrine of sanctification. Sanctification is the process whereby the believer's life is brought into harmony with God's will. The Reformers were concerned to distinguish between justification and sanctification because they wanted to avoid any danger of presenting the sanctified life as a prerequisite for justification. Sanctification depends upon justification, but justification never depends upon sanctification.

However, there were some dangers in dividing between justification and sanctification. Throughout the history of Protestantism there has been a tendency to divide the two themes so that justification is seen as something that has happened once in the past life of the Christian, while sanctification is a continuing activity throughout life. Related to this has been a tendency to see justification as what God has done for us while sanctification is what we are to do for God in gratitude for what he has done.

To escape these dangers, it must be seen that for the

Reformers, justification was a day-by-day, or better, a
moment-by-moment relationship with God. It is never the
case that we have been justified at some past time; we are
being continuously justified. We never grow so perfectly in
our sanctification that we no longer need to seek again the
loving forgiveness of God. We are ever in need of the
comforting words of the gospel with their good news of
God's graciousness toward us. Along the same lines,
sanctification cannot be our work for God, because any
newness of life that we achieve is dependent at every step
upon the relationship with God. In its own way, sanctification is as much a gift of God as is justification. We are
sanctified by grace alone through faith alone.

Sanctification arises from the Christian's relationship with
God, a relationship that has been established through
justification. Christians who have come to love God because God first loved them will naturally desire to do the
will of God. This means that they must seek to know God's
will for them. Historically this has raised the question of the
place of the law in the life of the Christian.

At the time of the Reformation the Reformers wrestled
with the question of the proper relationship between law
and gospel. They did not find it easy to answer this
question. Luther could say, "There's no man living on earth
who knows how to distinguish between the law and the
gospel . . . only the Holy Spirit knows this." [39] This
difficulty was illustrated when the Reformers failed to agree
completely upon the question of how many uses there were
for the law.

The Uses of the Law

It was agreed by the Reformers that there were at least
two uses of the law. First, the law was given by God so that

people might be made aware of their sin and helplessness and thus be led to turn to Christ for help. The forgiveness of sins could not be good news to someone who was not aware of any need of being forgiven. Thus Calvin, summing up the first use of the law, says: "For in the precepts of the law, God appears only, on the one hand, as the rewarder of perfect righteousness, of which we are all destitute; and on the other, as the severe judge of transgressions. But in Christ, his face shines with a plenitude of grace and lenity, even towards miserable and unworthy sinners." [40] The person who takes seriously the law of God with its demand for complete righteousness will be forced to confess his need of grace and forgiveness. Thus the law prepares the hearts of its hearers for the reception of the gospel.

In the second place, the law is given to maintain general order in society by causing those who otherwise have no concern for justice and rectitude, "when they hear its terrible sanctions, to be at least restrained by a fear of its penalties." [41] This was called the "civil use" of the law. Because the human race is sinful, self-centered, and given to injustice, there is the need for the law to provide external motivations that will result in a relative law and order for community life. As such the law obviously appears in the laws passed and enforced by governments, but it also appears in the powers of public opinion that act as pressures upon people to conduct their lives with relative decorum for fear of becoming social outcasts. This second use of the law was not seen by the Reformers as dependent upon the Biblical revelation. Human beings, as human beings, are moral creatures and have a sense of right and wrong that is not too far from the precepts of the Ten Commandments. The Reformers would have been impatient with the popular argument often heard for Christianity which claims that we need to be Christian (or at least religious) in order to have ethics. The Reformers knew that it is human nature to have ethics and that people, quite apart from any religious faith, could and would build relatively orderly societies.

While the Reformers were agreed that human beings, as human beings, are capable of a "civil righteousness" and that human governments are able to maintain law and order without religious aids, they insisted that this civil obedience did not lead to righteousness in God's eyes. The law-abiding citizens are simply acting out of prudence, avoiding the penalties of the state or the disdain of their neighbors. The second use of the law, therefore, cannot directly aid in salvation or justification. Since it results in relative law and order, it can provide a peaceful and orderly climate in which the gospel can be preached, but this is its sole contribution to salvation.

The question arises whether there is a third use of the law. Calvin, having summarized the first two uses of the law, went on to affirm that there is a third use, which is "the principal one." [42] This is a use of the law that applies only to Christians, among whom it has two functions. First, inasmuch as Christians desire to do the will of God, they need to know what is his will, and the law is the revelation of what God wills the Christian to do. But Calvin believed that there is need for more than instruction; the Christian also needs exhortation. Even God's saints are burdened with the "indolence of the flesh" and thus inclined to flag in their zeal for doing the will of God. Calvin concluded: "To this flesh the law serves as a whip, urging it, like a dull and tardy animal, forwards to its work; and even to the spiritual man, who is not yet delivered from the burden of the flesh, it will be a perpetual spur, that will not permit him to loiter." [43]

It seems clear that Luther did not believe in the third use of the law as we find it in Calvin. In the Smalcald Articles, which form part of the Confessions of the Lutheran churches, Luther mentions only two uses of the law.[44] However, the third use of the law is taught in the Formula of Concord, the last document included in the Lutheran Confessions, written over thirty years after Luther's death. A key passage reads: "On account of this Old Adam who inheres in people's intellect, will and all their powers, it is necessary for the law of God constantly to light their way lest in their merely human devotion they undertake self-decreed and self-chosen acts of serving God. This is further necessary lest the Old Adam go his own self-willed way. He must be coerced against his own will not only by the admonitions and threats of the law, but also by its punishments and plagues."[45] It will be noted that this argument parallels Calvin's very closely. For the Formula, as for Calvin, the third use of the law includes both instruction in what the will of God is and a goad to the weak flesh of the Christian to stir him to do more of the will of God than would be done if the Christian were left to the inner inclinations of the heart.

This debate over the third use of the law is more than a theoretical matter. One thing that keeps Lutheran churches divided in North America is the status given the Formula of Concord within the confessions of the church. Some Lutherans insist that all parts of the Book of Concord must be taken as of equal authority. Others insist that the Formula of Concord must be given less importance than the Augsburg Confession and Luther's Small Catechism. An important reason why some Lutherans have hesitation about accepting the Formula of Concord is that it teaches the third use of the law. But, quite apart from the inner problems of Lutheranism, the third use of the law has important consequences for the life of Protestant churches.

A major thesis that I have been presenting is that many

Protestants believe in salvation by works because the practice of Protestant churches has spoken more loudly than their preaching of justification. But if we accept the third use of the law, we could justify many of these practices. For example, the rules enforced in institutions of the church could be defended as necessary to goad the indolent flesh of Christians in those institutions. It is important, therefore, to examine closely whether we should restructure our doctrine of justification based on the third use of the law or whether a proper understanding of justification precludes the third use.

The first problem in evaluating the positions on the relationship of law and gospel is that the term "law" is not always used to mean the same thing. Gerhard Ebeling points out that although Luther's use of the "law" is derived from Biblical usage, nonetheless "for historical and practical reasons the Pauline concept of the law is not simply identical with that of the Old Testament; and in its turn, Luther's concept of the law is not simply identical with that of St. Paul." [46] It is thus necessary to begin our discussion with a rather careful definition of how we are using the term "law."

At one level we may think of the law as simply God's revelation of his will. In Ps. 40:8 we read, "I delight to do thy will, O my God; thy law is within my heart." Here the law is synonymous with God's revealed will. The psalmist is in that relationship with God which we have described as justification by grace through faith, and thus he delights to do God's will (i.e., law) and he bears it in his heart. When, however, Paul tells the Christians that they are no longer under the law (Rom. 6:14) he obviously means more by law than the revealed will of God. Paul is not telling Christians that they are no longer under God's revealed will.

As we read the Fortieth Psalm, we see clearly a long

hymn of the gospel. Standing within the chosen people of
God, the psalmist is keenly aware of all that God has
graciously done for his people. "Thou hast multiplied, O
LORD my God, thy wondrous deeds and thy thoughts
toward us" (Ps. 40:5). Furthermore, the psalmist is aware of
God's love for him personally: "He drew me up from the
desolate pit, out of the miry bog, and set my feet upon a
rock, making my steps secure" (Ps. 40:2). The psalmist
answers God's love with a responding love that longs to
please God and thus, for him, God's law means simply what
God wills.

Paul, however, is writing against a different historical
background. A religious tradition has grown up that
identifies the law as a series of rules and regulations to be
followed whereby people can make themselves righteous in
the sight of God and the community. As such, the law has
become a burden upon the people. If they fail to keep the
law, they are under the threat of God's punishment, here
and hereafter, and they are despised by the religious elite as
sinners. If they keep the law, they are puffed up in pride
and thank God they are not as others. Where law has such
connotations, the gospel can only mean the good news that
God's forgiving love comes to people regardless of their
merits. Thus Paul can assure them that they are no longer
under the law. In each of his epistles Paul concludes with
ethical exhortations to his readers. He expects that they will
wish to do God's will. But, because of the connotations of
the term "law" in Paul's time, he cannot, as did the
psalmist, refer to these items of God's will as the law.

Luther began from Paul's use of the term "law," but more
history had occurred to give further connotations to the
term. The medieval church, with its emphasis upon purgatory, had preached a system of good works whereby people
could escape from or lessen the time of suffering in

purgatory. They were preoccupied with building up merits to offset their demerits. At its worst, the medieval church turned the relationship of God and his people into a commercial affair in which, through indulgences, salvation could be bought not simply with good works but with money. When Luther speaks of the law, he uses the term consistently to imply those actions imposed upon persons with an accompanying threat of punishment and hope of reward.

At first sight it would appear that Luther should have no problem in separating law and gospel, given his definition of law. And at times he makes a relatively simple distinction. Thus he can say that "the entire Scripture of God is divided into two parts: commandments and promises." [47] It would seem that this distinction would enable one to go through Scripture and distinguish law and gospel rather simply. Where commandments are found and the requirements of God's will are laid upon us, there is law. But where there are promises of God's grace and forgiveness and the new life in Christ, there is gospel. Why then does Luther say, as quoted above, that no man living can distinguish law and gospel but that only the Holy Spirit can do it? The answer is that for Luther law and gospel are not simply objective facts about Scripture. The same passage of Scripture may be either law or gospel, depending upon who reads it or how it is preached. Thus for Luther, Christ is simply and purely gospel; but Luther found that the medieval church had used Christ as a law. He says, "In our day we are taught by the doctrine of men to seek nothing but merits, rewards, and the things that are ours; of Christ we have made only a taskmaster far harsher than Moses." [48] On the other hand, to a person seeking to express love to God, it may be pure gospel to find a Biblical passage that declares what God wills to have done.

For Luther, wherever the Scripture is approached and read in terms of rules whereby one may escape punishment or reap reward, there is law. But when Scripture is read with a loving response to God's grace, there is gospel. The reason why only the Holy Spirit can finally distinguish law and gospel is that we can never be certain of our own hearts. Luther asks, "For who knows whether or not he is acting out of fear or a love for his own convenience even in a very subtle manner in his devotional life and his good works, looking for rest and a reward rather than the will of God?" [49] Because self-centered humans can turn the good news of God's grace into self-seeking law, it is ultimately only the Holy Spirit who can say where law and where gospel are actually operating.

With Luther's use of the terms "law" and "gospel," the first thing that he would probably say about the third use of the law is that it is a logical impossibility. Both Calvin and the authors of the Formula of Concord see two aspects under the third use of the law. First, the law is guidance as to the will of God for the Christian who has been filled with a desire to do God's will. For Luther this would be no longer "law" at all. Inasmuch as the Christian is searching the Scripture to find God's will because he longs to do God's will, it comes under gospel and not law. The attitude of the Christian joyfully seeking God's will that he might do it is quite the opposite of the attitude of the fear-filled person to whom God's will is law. The other aspect of the third use is to coerce the Old Adam or to be a whip to the lazy flesh. To Luther, however, this would be simply the first use of the law.

Luther emphasized that the Christian remains at one and the same time justified and a forgiven sinner. Daily the Christian needs to relive his baptism in which he dies to sin and is raised with Christ. Justification is thus not a

once-and-for-all event that the Christian has in his past, it is
a moment-by-moment renewal of his relationship with God.
Therefore, insofar as the justified one is still sinner, he hears
the Word of God's commands as a coercive whip. But what
is the Christian's proper response? It cannot be to give a
legalistic and painful obedience; rather, it is to turn again to
the good news of forgiveness. In short, the first use of the
law is to bring people to see their need of Christ and that is
all that can be accomplished by the so-called third use of
the law.

Saying that for Luther a third use of the law is a logical
impossibility is to say that, given Luther's use of the word
"law," the so-called third use would be incorporated in the
first two. It still remains possible that, given a somewhat
different use of the term "law," a third use may be logically
possible. Is it the case that Calvin and the Formula of
Concord are using the term somewhat differently? If so,
there may be no disagreement between Luther and these
later views.

It is not easy to answer this question, because neither
Calvin nor the Formula is as clear as we might wish. When
Calvin speaks of the law as a whip to the flesh of the
Christian, it seems that he is sanctioning a use of the law for
the Christian that Luther would find repugnant. However,
as we continue reading this section of Calvin, we are not
sure. Immediately after his words about the law as a whip
he goes on to illustrate his point by reference to the psalms
where the law is seen as a delight and joy. And he can say:
"For Moses has abundantly taught us, that the law, which in
sinners can only produce death, ought to have a better and
more excellent use in the saints." [50] Again, he explains that
the law has been abrogated for Christians in that "it ceases
to be to them what it was before, no longer terrifying and
confounding their consciences, condemning and destroying

them." [51] And so he concludes that for Paul the law has not been abrogated as instruction but as a power of binding the conscience.[52] This seems to be in harmony with Luther's concern. But if so, Calvin's earlier words about it being a whip to the flesh of the Christian are unfortunately misleading.

We have a similar problem with the Formula of Concord. Having spoken of the third use of the law in terms of coercing the Old Adam in us, the Formula goes on to affirm that works are works of the law "as long as they are extorted from people only under the coercion of punishments and the threat of God's wrath." As such they are distinguished from works of the spirit, which the Christians "perform in so far as they are reborn and do them as spontaneously as if they knew of no command." [53] From this the Formula concludes that God's children are not under law but under grace, all of which leaves us somewhat confused as to whether or not the Formula is proposing a use of the law that would be at odds with Luther.

Insofar as the third use of the law implies that the threat of the law must be kept over the Christian to coerce the Old Adam or to whip the lazy flesh, it is a serious distortion of what is at stake in justification by grace alone through faith alone. If it has been correct to argue that justification looks to the righteousness of the heart and hence to motivation rather than ethical behaviorism, then it cannot be legitimate to return to such a use of law for the Christian. Likewise, insofar as justification means the liberation from the bondage of being curved in upon ourselves, such a use of the law leads back to a new bondage.

Luther saw this clearly. Again and again through his writings he emphasizes that what is done through fear of punishment or hope of reward is of no significance for the righteousness of the Christian. For example, he says that

Satan deceives some "in this way, that they do not see their own weaknesses and the inclination of their wicked will, nor have they analyzed themselves to see how unwillingly they obey the law and how little they love it, but actually they believe and act out of a servile fear; yet they think that they are doing enough and that they must therefore be regarded as righteous before God, because they believe and act; yet they are in no way anxious to do this work so as to do it gladly in joy and love and with full will, or even to see their need of God's grace to accomplish it." [54] In this passage Luther states that so long as the law is obeyed because of consequences, it falls short of the righteousness to which God calls the Christian. But, if threats are powerless, it is no better to take the opposite approach and hold forth the rewards of righteousness. Speaking of those people who do good deeds in order to gain glory and repayment "both temporal and eternal," Luther says: "For they do not give in simplicity for the glory of God but for the sake of their own future advantage in heaven, and they would not make the gift if it were not for their hope of this advantage. But it is in vain, for they are double-minded." [55]

It is clear why Luther, defining law as commandments that come to us with the sanctions of threats and rewards, could not see a third use of the law for the Christian. To preach the law to one who has been freed by love from self-centered preoccupation with himself would be to encourage backsliding into the state from which grace had freed him. With some pessimism Luther suggests that if fear were removed as an incentive for attending church services and other church activities, all churches would close within a year. But he affirms, "And yet so it ought to be, and we should approach all of these things as people about to serve God freely and happily and not out of fear of conscience or punishment, nor in the hope of reward or honor." [56] If Luther was ready to let the churches close rather than to preach fear about not attending, he was not ready to make a third use of the law to spur Christians into greater activity.

God's Will for the Christian's Life

But the term "law" does have another meaning. For the psalmist the law meant simply the revealed will of God. There is a continuing use of the law in this sense for the justified Christian. Since it is of the nature of justification to motivate the believer to desire to do God's will, it becomes necessary for the believer to ask what the will of God is. In part, at least, this is what Calvin and the Formula of Concord are advocating in the third use of the law. Although Luther would not use the term "law" in this context, he would agree with the intent. In his catechisms he expounded the Ten Commandments as guides for Christian life. In introducing his sermons on the Sermon on the Mount, he heaps scorn on those who claim that "Christ does not intend everything he teaches in the fifth chapter [of Matthew] to be regarded by his Christians as a command for them to observe." [57] Luther believed that the Christian believer, filled with a desire to do God's will, would seek to find that will, and his search would begin with God's revelation in the Scriptures.

It has been our thesis throughout this work that the doctrine of justification is rooted in the teachings of Jesus. If this is the case, then the justified person who is seeking to know the will of God ought to begin with the life and teachings of Jesus. While this is not the time and place to develop a doctrine of sanctification or a complete Christian ethic, we need to see something of the direction in which the justified Christian is led by Jesus.

When asked what was the great commandment of the law, Jesus answered: "You shall love the Lord your God with all your heart, and with all your soul, and with all your mind. This is the great and first commandment. And the second is like it, You shall love your neighbor as yourself. On these two commandments depend all the law and the prophets." (Matt. 22:37–40.) This is the answer that we would expect in the light of justification. God reveals himself as the forgiving father who seeks his lost children, and his love awakens a responding love in their hearts. Could the will of God be anything but that we should love others even as he has loved us?

Here we find another reason why many Christians object to the use of the term "law" to refer to God's will for the Christian. For many people the term "law" brings to mind a series of unbending rules and regulations that must be obeyed regardless of consequences. To be under the law is to be in bondage to a system of such rules and regulations. When Jesus summed up all the commandments in terms of the two commandments to love God and the neighbor, he freed his followers from bondage to inflexible rules. A major reason for the opposition of the religious leaders to Jesus was the willingness of Jesus to break their cultic laws when love called for it. If law is defined in terms of inflexible rules and regulations, the Christian is not under the law; Jesus makes clear that the Christian is to be guided by love and not by legalistic rules.

For many people it is frightening to have the law summed up in terms of love. So long as we live by rules and regulations we know exactly what is right and what is wrong; we can keep track of our progress in sanctification. Certainly, so long as we live by a works-righteousness that assumes that we must make ourselves worthy, we dare not give up the security of the rules that tell us in advance how

we must act. Only when we have understood the full
implications of justification will we dare to accept love of
God and neighbor as our guides for decision. Then we shall
have to weigh the implications of the situation before us and
attempt to see how love can best be expressed within it.
Because life is seldom simple, we shall face many situations
in which we cannot be sure that we have chosen the most
loving way of acting. In such cases we must act in
confidence that God's forgiveness is not dependent upon
the wisdom with which we choose the action to be
performed.

Joseph Fletcher, in developing his situational ethics, has
attempted to give the Christian guidance in making choices
in the light of love. He suggests that we need to work out
an "agapeic calculus" by which we can weigh each situation
to see what actions will maximize love and thus achieve
"the greatest amount of neighbor welfare for the largest
number of neighbors possible." [58] But it is doubtful that
such a calculus can do justice to Christian love. In the
agonizing choices of life, how do we weigh love to one
person against love to another? Does a little love expressed
to each of a hundred people add up to more than a great
deal of love to a single person? Fletcher says that President
Truman made his decision to drop the atomic bombs on
Japan on the basis of an agapeic calculus.[59] Quite obviously
in Truman's calculations an American life weighed a great
deal more than a Japanese life.

Even if it is granted that all lives have an equal value in
working out the agapeic calculus, is it a legitimate way of
expressing the meaning of Christian love? Recently in
Canada there was an illustration of agapeic calculus in
action. The Province of Quebec had begun a six billion
dollar hydroelectric project in the Northern region of James
Bay. The native peoples of the region, Indians and Eskimos,

instigated a court case against the project charging that it was destroying their way of life and violating their rights to the land of the region. After a long hearing, a Superior Court judge granted an injunction against the continuance of the work until the case could be finally settled in court. This created considerable consternation, inasmuch as it was costing an astronomical amount of money each day that the work was stopped. An appeal was launched and a quick decision came down from the Court of Appeal allowing the work to go forward. The reason given was that the interests of the few thousand native people involved "do not bear comparison" to the interests of the 6,000,000 people of Quebec. This is in keeping with Fletcher's agapeic calculus, since it brought about the greatest amount of neighbor welfare for the largest number of neighbors possible. But was it love? The lawyers for the native people appealed the case, charging that the decision of the Court of Appeal had been made on the principle of "might makes right." They had a good point, and it brings out the failure of an agapeic calculus to distribute love in a loving way.

The Nature of Christian Love

If Jesus' admonition to love one's neighbors is to be applied, the meaning of love in the Scriptures must be examined. For the Scriptures, the nature of love is defined by the form of love that God expresses. The doctrine of justification is rooted in God's concern for all persons. He is not content with ninety-nine safely in the fold, he must seek for the lost one. He numbers the hairs of each head (Luke 12:7). Therefore, it is God's will that we should express love to all persons. When the good Samaritan found the man who had fallen among thieves, he acted to meet the immediate needs of the man (Luke 10:29–37). We are not told how the Samaritan felt about the wounded man. Assuming that the man was a Jew, the agelong tension between Jews and Samaritans would no doubt affect his feelings. But he acted as a good neighbor to do what was in his power to meet the other's needs. That is what Christian love is all about.

But we can go farther. The God who seeks the lost has a special concern for the down-and-out, for the weak and the helpless. Luke tells us that at the beginning of his ministry Jesus defined that ministry by quoting from Isaiah: "The Spirit of the Lord is upon me, because he has anointed me to preach good news to the poor. He has sent me to proclaim release to the captives and recovering of sight to the blind, to set at liberty those who are oppressed, to proclaim the acceptable year of the Lord." (Luke 4:18–19.) James Cone is fully justified in taking this passage as the beginning of his black theology of liberation. The God revealed in Jesus is a God who is concerned with the poor, those held in bondage, the blind, and those who are oppressed. As Cone points out, this is a special word to the ghetto.[60] This is a vision of love which, in terms of the example given above, would not weigh the interests of 6,000,000 people as obviously taking precedence over the interests of a few thousand native people. On the contrary, because the native people are few and weak, they need special rights and they need protection from the power of the majority. From the prophets of the Old Testament to Jesus, the love of God is portrayed as having a particular concern with widows and orphans, the poor and the oppressed, the despised and outcast groups of society.

God's love is not the sentimental attitude that is often in our time identified as love. There is steel in God's love. Precisely because God does love the poor and the oppressed, there is wrath toward those who exploit the weak.

Jesus can say that it is better for a man to have a millstone hung around his neck and to be cast into the sea than to be guilty of causing a "little one" to stumble (Luke 17:2). Mary, in the Magnificat, pondering the coming birth of Jesus, sees God as putting down the mighty from their thrones and filling the hungry with good things, while sending the rich away empty (Luke 1:52–53). Jesus cleansed the Temple with obvious anger against the powerful group that had taken over the court where Gentiles could worship the God of Abraham, Isaac, and Jacob and had turned it into a "den of robbers" (Luke 19:45–46). This last phrase indicates that Jesus was angry at the way in which the authorities were using their monopoly power to exploit the people who came to the Temple to worship.

One of the ways in which Jesus expressed special concern for the oppressed is found in his treatment of women. In the world of Jesus' time women held a position equivalent to slavery. Perhaps the lot of women was somewhat better among the Jews than among Greeks or Romans, but even so the pious Jewish male had good reason for his daily prayer in which he thanked God that he had not been born a woman. A wife could be divorced on the whim of her husband, but she could not divorce him, whatever his offense. Unless a woman was kept in the house of her father or her husband, she had no way to live except through prostitution. Many rabbis refused to speak to a woman in public. When the worshipers were counted to see if there was a quorum, women did not count, for women were able to worship only through their husbands. When Mary marveled that God had regard for "the low estate of his handmaiden" (Luke 1:48) she was referring to her place in society as a woman.

Against this background we find that Jesus treated women as equals. When he was visiting in the home of

Mary and Martha, Martha fell into the role assigned to women—working in the kitchen to wait on the male. Meanwhile Mary was in the shocking role of talking seriously with Jesus. Martha called upon Jesus to tell Mary to help in the serving. But Jesus, who was treating Mary as a person and not as a second-class citizen, rebuked Martha for her concerns. The rebuke was gentle and kindly because Jesus knew that Martha was the product of her culture. Nonetheless, he told her, "Mary has chosen the good portion, which shall not be taken away from her" (Luke 10:42). In these words Jesus was freeing women from the captivity into which their culture had placed them. Women were among Jesus' disciples, and no doubt this was one of the reasons for the official opposition to Jesus. On one occasion the disciples were shocked to find Jesus talking publicly not only with a woman but with one who was of dubious virtue (John 4:27). Yet Jesus revealed to this woman his messiahship. It was no accident that it was the women to whom Jesus first appeared after his resurrection. Throughout his life he had defied his culture and treated this oppressed group as equally the children of God with their male oppressors. It remains a major irony that it has taken the Christian church nearly twenty centuries to recognize the significance of Jesus' attitude toward women. Even today the position of women in the church is usually limited more to the role of Martha than to the role of Mary.

In centering upon love as the heart of God's will for his followers, Jesus brought out another point that is highly relevant to the doctrine of justification. It seems to be a rule of the religious life that where it is believed that people must save themselves by good works, the works whereby they try to save themselves inevitably become religious acts rather than service to persons. Jesus was continually in conflict with the religious leadership of his time because he was not as concerned as they with the niceties of religious practice. He and his disciples were attacked because they could not be bothered to go through the religious ceremony of dipping their hands in water before eating (Mark 7:1–5). Jesus also took a casual attitude to the rules that had been developed to observe the Sabbath. He was unconcerned when his disciples "threshed wheat" on the Sabbath (Luke 6:1–5). He continuously shocked the authorities by healing on the Sabbath. On one of these occasions he responded by telling his critics that the Sabbath was made for man and not man for the Sabbath (Mark 2:23–28).

In insisting that the Sabbath observance should be for the sake of human need and not a meticulous performance to make oneself righteous, Jesus was bringing out the implications of summarizing the law in the twofold command to love God and neighbor. Works-righteousness is always concerned with the saving of oneself. The person who is curved in upon himself is first of all concerned with what can be done for his own benefit. When such a person thinks of God he naturally creates God in his own image. He therefore assumes that what will be most pleasing to God will be actions directed toward God himself. The best way of pleasing God will then seem to be to perform religious acts that are centered upon God's majesty, honor, and so on. The careful observance of the Sabbath is an obvious way of paying homage to God, so surely this will be most pleasing to God. But the God who justifies by grace through faith is a God of love, and he is most concerned with others. He is more pleased by service to the neighbor than by service to himself. This is why God created the Sabbath for man and not man for the Sabbath. The purpose of the Sabbath is not to gratify God's self-interest but to serve the need of humanity. Thus healing the sick on the Sabbath is actually the finest form of keeping it.

At the time of the Reformation, the good works whereby salvation was to be sought were almost exclusively actions that had no concern for the neighbor. Good works were praying, going into monasteries to live, buying indulgences, building church buildings, and so on. In deploring this kind of good works, Luther commented that "all the legitimate good works instituted and ordered by God were despised and even reduced to nothing, such as the work of a ruler, subject, father, mother, son, daughter, servant, and maid. They were not called good works and did not belong to penance either, but were known as a 'secular existence,' a 'perilous estate,' and 'lost works.' " [61] Here Luther's understanding of justification has led him to see that the works which are truly good in God's eyes are works which serve our neighbors rather than works in performance of religious formalities. Commenting on Phil. 2:1–4, Luther says that Paul "has prescribed this rule for the life of Christians, namely that we should devote all our works to the welfare of others, since each has such abundant riches in his faith that all his other works and his whole life are a surplus with which he can by voluntary benevolence serve and do good to his neighbor." [62]

In the first chapter of this book we argued that one of the reasons Protestants do not really believe in justification by grace through faith is that Protestant churches define active church membership almost exclusively in terms of activities within the church organization. We quoted Langdon Gilkey to the effect that this was an excellent medieval "works" definition. Now we are able to see more clearly why this is so. The relationship with God that flows from justification frees the person to love his neighbor. But works-righteousness, by its very nature, seeks to perform religious acts directed toward God in the hope of winning God's favor and turning aside his wrath. When churches put their prime emphasis upon activities within the institutional structure of the church, and when the primary tests of active membership are attendance at worship services and the giving of money to the church, then inevitably the practice of the church is teaching a works-righteousness. No matter how soundly it preaches justification, its actions will speak louder than its words.

The same problem is implicit in the tendency of Protestant churches to put a major emphasis upon personal behavior. When Protestants seek to influence legislation, they all too often seek laws that would make people personally righteous. They seek prohibition of liquor or drugs, censorship of pornography, laws against gambling, prostitution, homosexuality, and so on. Seeking such laws makes it appear that Protestants are more concerned with forcing individuals to behave themselves than they are with expressing love to the poor, the weak, and the dispossessed. Once more practice has blurred the meaning of justification so that what is said cannot be heard. At the heart of understanding justification is the recognition that God's will calls us to act in love toward our neighbors even as God loves them. In the parable of the sheep and the goats, Jesus could picture the final judgment of God in terms of actions of love to the poor and needy (Matt. 25:31–46). At first sight this parable may appear to be a parable of salvation by works. Those who are judged righteous are those who have fed the hungry, clothed the naked, and so on. It may seem we should hunt up the hungry to feed them so that we can save our own souls. But a key part of the parable is that both sheep and goats are surprised to find that Jesus sees their actions as having been done to him. The hungry were fed out of love and concern for them and not for any self-seeking reasons. So seen, this parable brings out the implication of justification. It means that the person in this relationship to God is one who spontaneously will act to meet the needs of others. When the actions of the churches make it appear that they are more concerned with personal righteousness than with love to the neighbor, the doctrine of justification loses its credibility.

At the center of God's will, seen through the doctrine of justification, is God's willingness to forgive. In an earlier chapter this was examined, and it was seen that the forgiven ones are called upon to forgive. Here it can be emphasized again in the light of God's will, which the justified are seeking to fulfill. Jesus makes it clear in his teachings that God calls us to forgive. On one occasion Peter came to Jesus and asked how often he should forgive one who had sinned against him (Matt. 18:21). No doubt Peter felt he was being generous when he suggested seven times. In the everyday world in which we live we would have to confess that anyone who forgave another seven times would have to be regarded as going the second mile. We might forgive an offender once or twice, but if he went on repeating the offense, most of us would decide that he was not repentant and thus not worthy of being forgiven a seventh time. Jesus did not see it this way: "I do not say to you seven times, but seventy times seven" (Matt. 18:22). This does not mean that we should forgive four hundred and ninety times. It means that our forgiveness should flow freely without limit.

Here once again the practice of the churches speaks louder than what they say. If churches do not practice forgiveness, how can they expect people to believe that God forgives? And if we do not believe that God freely forgives, then the doctrine of justification by grace through faith becomes incredible.

As I write, there comes to my desk a news release which reports a survey made by the president of one of the leading United States denominations. The denomination shall be left nameless because we have no reason to think that its attitudes are significantly different from that of others. The survey indicated that the membership of the church opposed by a 2–1 majority granting amnesty to those who left the United States rather than to serve in the armed forces during the Vietnam war. Looked at from outside the United States, this question does not appear to be a matter of forgiveness. One thing that allowed some of us to keep faith in the United States during the shameful interlude of the Vietnam war was the saving remnant of Americans who chose exile rather than to take part in that war. However, if we can grant the premise that such people did something wrong, we have to ask what it means when church people vote 2–1 against forgiving them. The church involved in this survey is a stalwart preacher of justification. How can we believe its teaching when its people are filled with a spirit of vengeance rather than a willingness to forgive?

In these last few pages an attempt has been made to show what is involved in seeking the will of God in the light of justification. It has been emphasized that God's will must be sought in the light of the nature of God revealed in the fact that God justifies by his grace and not by the works of people. Given some definitions of law, this could be called a third use of the law. But, given other definitions of law, this would be brought under gospel rather than law.

Law and Gospel

Perhaps it is a matter of semantics whether or not we find a third use of the law in the life of the Christian. If we agree that there is no place in the life of the Christian for the law in the sense of rules that come with promises of rewards or threats of punishment, it may be relatively harmless to use the term "law" to refer to the will of God,

which the justified Christian will naturally seek to find. But
a matter of semantics can be important. We have seen that
the tradition of using "justification by faith alone" as the
term for "justification by grace alone through faith alone"
has had connotations that have misled many into misunderstanding the doctrine. Because of the nature of God's will,
which we have seen in the light of justification, it appears
that the term "law" may have some seriously misleading
connotations.

For one thing, the term "law" almost inevitably calls to
mind the legal context where laws must be obeyed or else.
To speak of God's will for the Christian as God's law is to
invite us to assume that the Christian remains under the
legalistic rewards-and-punishment relationship with God.
Furthermore, "law" does bear the connotation of hard and-
fast rules and regulations that, in advance of all situations,
inform us of those things which must always be done. Such
a connotation cannot do justice to the goal of love to God
and neighbor, which Jesus set forth as the center of God's
will for his children. It seems desirable to use some term
other than law to describe God's will for the Christian life.

Paul Althaus has suggested that we use the term "the
divine command" to describe the original form of God's will
for humanity which was distorted by sin into "law." [63] At
first sight, I must confess, the term "command" did not
appeal to me as being any better than "law." However,
there is a Biblical precedent for this distinction of terms. In
John's Gospel, virtually every time that *nomos* ("law") is
used it refers to the Old Testament law or to the practice of
the religious establishment in Jerusalem during Jesus' life.
On the other hand when, in John's Gospel, Jesus exhorts his
disciples to good works, the term *nomos* is never used;
instead we find the term *entolas* ("commandments"). In
this way "the law" refers to the old order, where God's will

was seen in terms of condemnation, while "commandment" is within the context of the gospel. John's Prologue gives the basis for this distinction when he says, "For the law was given through Moses; grace and truth came through Jesus Christ" (John 1:17).

The difference between the law and commandment comes out when Jesus says, "A new commandment I give to you, that you love one another; even as I have loved you, that you also love one another" (John 13:34). This commandment is new when compared to the law. It does not consist of laying down rules and regulations but calls the disciples to pattern themselves after the life and actions of Jesus. The new commandment does not relate the disciples to a law but to a person, Jesus himself. Furthermore, the motivation is clearly not prudential in any sense; the disciples are to love one another because Jesus has loved them. The same point comes out again in the next chapter, where Jesus says, "If you love me, you will keep my commandments" (John 14:15). The law, by contrast, always says: If you will keep my commandments, I will love you. The Christian life, lived in the light of justification, always operates from the theme that we do God's will, not in order that God will love us, but because God first loves us and because he has inspired in our hearts an answering love.

VII

Evangelism and the First Use of the Law

ONE OF THE REASONS why the Protestant preaching of justification is not believed is that much of our evangelism is geared to the theme that people ought to become Christian "because it is good for you." This means that evangelism is appealing to the very curved-in-upon-oneself condition from which it is the goal of Christian faith to deliver us. But, we may ask, if people are centered in themselves, must not our evangelism begin by appealing to their self-interest? Can we expect the self-centered to embrace Christianity if we cannot answer the question, What's in it for me? Must we not begin with the selfish appeal in the hope that growth in Christian faith will bring the converts to a more selfless understanding?

The First Use of the Law in the Reformation

Questions such as these require a look at the first use of the law. The law, in the sense of the demands that come to us with threats of punishment and promise of rewards, has no place in the life of the Christian. But does it have a place in bringing a person to Christian faith? The Reformers believed that the law plays a role in evangelism. They took as their starting point Gal. 3:23–26, where Paul likens the law to the custodian or tutor who had the task of taking a child to school. As the custodian's task is finished when the child arrives at school, so the law has completed its task when a person is brought to Christ. The law cannot save anyone; nonetheless, it does perform an important role in salvation.

The law brings us to Christ, the Reformers believed, because it reveals to us our hopelessness apart from God's grace. Luther put it thus: "Therefore the true function and the chief and proper use of the Law is to reveal to man his sin, blindness, misery, wickedness, ignorance, hate and contempt of God, death, hell, judgment, and the well deserved wrath of God." [64] Luther and Calvin agreed that the law cannot bring salvation because no one is able to fulfill the full demands of the law. God calls upon us to be perfect as he is perfect, and we all fall short of that. By itself the law can only be a source of hopelessness. Calvin stated it this way: "Therefore, if we direct our views exclusively to the law, the effects upon our minds will only be despondency, confusion, and despair, since it condemns and curses us all, and keeps us far from that blessedness which it proposes to them who observe it." [65] However, Calvin goes on to affirm that it is not God's intention in the law to make us feel despondent. On the contrary, the law serves as a dark background against which God's grace appears even more bright.[66]

Protestant churches traditionally drew the conclusion from the Reformers that effective evangelism should first preach the law in the sense of filling people with a fear of hell. Then, at the point where fear has gripped the hearers, the words of grace can be proclaimed and the fear-stricken hearers will gratefully accept the offer of grace. The traditional revival meeting was constructed along just those lines. In a later, more secularized period, emphasis has shifted from hell in an afterlife to the basic unhappiness of unbelievers in this life. Thus existentialist philosophies of gloom or the theater of the absurd have been used to picture the meaninglessness of existence apart from faith. Bonhoeffer called such an approach "secularized Methodism" and ridiculed those who attempt to "demonstrate to secure, contented, happy mankind that it is really unhappy and desperate, and merely unwilling to realize that it is in severe straits it knows nothing at all about." [67]

Bonhoeffer felt that such an approach was futile in the modern world because it could only persuade a small number of "degenerates" who had an inflated concern with themselves. But, worse still, he felt that it was ignoble because it was an attempt by Christianity to exploit the weakness of people. In addition to Bonhoeffer's critique it must be asked whether such an approach does not distort the meaning of justification. Inasmuch as such an approach begins by intensifying the self-concern of the hearer, can we hope that it will end up by liberating him from his bondage of being curved in upon himself? Can selfishness be overcome by appealing to selfishness?

It is not easy to determine whether or not Luther and Calvin would have agreed with the later interpretations of Protestants. We must recall the particular historical context in which they spoke. At the time of the Reformation the religious situation was complex. On the one hand, there seems to have been considerable indifference to religion and skepticism about its claims. This was evident inside the church, where many of the clergy used their position to acquire worldly wealth and comforts. Outside the church it was evident in the large numbers of people who were alienated from the church. On the other hand, the sixteenth century was a time when the hope of an afterlife was a very important reality for most people. To combat the indifference to the church, the practice grew up of using threats about the afterlife to spur the indifferent to do more for the church. This was successful; money poured in to buy indulgences, thousands went on pilgrimages to purify their souls, and a variety of fervent religious acts were popular as people tried to reduce the time they would have to spend in purgatory. As a result the Reformers did not have to raise the question as to whether or not they should stimulate fears about punishment. The fears were there, in their world, and to the fear-haunted people they could preach the good news that the just shall live by faith.

In short, for the Reformers, it was obvious that the law already had, in their time, awakened fear in the hearts of people. In so doing, it had prepared a way for some to respond to the gospel of Christ. We cannot be sure what the Reformers might say to an age such as ours in which few unbelievers seem to be worried about eternal punishment. Would they advocate preaching about eternal damnation in the attempt to create fear? Would they see the law operating in the meaninglessness and misery of modern life and proclaim that without faith there can be no escape from such miseries? It is not easy to answer such questions.

When the Jesus People appeared and were examined in the public media, there were some commentators who argued that they differed from orthodox Christianity in that they had little to say about sin or guilt. Their primary approach was to walk up to people and say, "God loves you." To say so little about sin, guilt, and punishment is to break from much of the history of orthodox Protestantism, but it might not have seemed so strange to Luther or Calvin. Both of them did express severe reservations about what could be achieved through an appeal to the self-interest of the potential convert. There can be no doubt that the Reformers believed that there was an eternal punishment for the Godless, but they had no great optimism that fear of this punishment would be an effective basis for evangelism.

In discussing how people come to faith, Calvin says that the human heart is by no means excited to faith by every word found in Scripture. God told Adam that he would surely die, and Cain was condemned by his brother's blood, but, says Calvin, "these declarations are so far from being adapted to the establishment of faith, that of themselves they can only shake it." [68] Calvin continues by saying that when our conscience beholds the vengeance of God, we cannot refrain from wanting to run away from God. But faith can only arise from seeking God, not by fleeing from him. Consequently, says Calvin, faith can only arise from those Biblical words that tell us of God's love and benevolence.

Luther agreed with this analysis by Calvin. The God who punishes can only instill fear in our hearts, and where we fear we must hate the cause of the fear. A typical statement by Luther is the following: "And this is the only way to achieve a true conversion, namely through love and kindness. For he who is converted through threats and terror is never truly converted as long as he retains that form of conversion. For fear makes him hate his conversion. But he who is converted by love is completely burned up against himself and is far more angry with himself than anyone else can be with him, and he is totally displeased with himself." [69] Luther here shows a profound insight into human psychology. If a person has been converted through fear, he will hate his conversion and God himself because he will feel that he has been bludgeoned into the faith. It is almost impossible for him to have the joy of freedom that is promised to the Christian.

Rewards and Punishments

These words of the Reformers reveal a dilemma. The law, preaching the fear of punishment, causes self-centered people to turn more vigorously in upon themselves. Filled with fear, they seek to know what they can do that they may escape that which they fear. When such people are told that they must have faith, inevitably they see faith as a work that they must perform in order to earn the remission of the penalty. But faith is not something that we can will to have. In an earlier chapter we saw that faith is basically a trustful giving of oneself in response to God's love. The Reformers quite profoundly described it as a gift, because it is born in the heart of a person in response to God's love. It is no more possible to have faith by an act of will than it is to wake up some morning and will to fall in love that day with some specified person. Where then does this leave the people who have been filled with fear of punishment? Inevitably they must think of faith in terms of believing something. They fall into the pattern of viewing a belief in doctrines as a good work that must be performed in order to save themselves. Fear has not brought such a person to faith.

It would seem that Jesus clearly repudiated the value of fear to bring people to faith. In the parable of the rich man and Lazarus we have the picture of the rich man in hell, conversing with Abraham. The rich man wants to send a messenger back to earth to warn his five brothers of the doom that awaits them if they do not mend their ways. He is quite sure that a voice from the dead, warning them of what is to come, will have a powerful motivating effect to change their lives. But Abraham answers, "If they do not hear Moses and the prophets, neither will they be convinced if someone should rise from the dead" (Luke 16:31). Jesus is saying in this parable that people will not be won to righteousness by being warned of the penalties that lie ahead of them.

If the Reformers agreed with Jesus that fear of punishments could not lead to faith, what did they mean when they spoke of the first use of the law as bringing people to Christ? Were they confused and mistaken? Did they fail to carry through justification at this point and thus leave a basis for the undermining of the doctrine in the later Protestant church? Before we decide that the Reformers were in error, we need to see that the terms "reward" and "punishment" are used with somewhat different meanings. Normally they mean certain extrinsic results of actions, but they can also point to intrinsic results of actions. When someone speaks of reward or punishment it is important to see which of these meanings is implied.

Extrinsic rewards or punishments are arbitrarily selected to motivate an action. For example, if parents give their son candy or money for practicing his piano lesson, it is an extrinsic reward because there is no intrinsic relationship between practicing a piano lesson and getting candy or money. The parents have arbitrarily chosen these rewards. If the son is not allowed to go to the movies when he fails to practice, it is an arbitrary punishment because there is no intrinsic relationship between failing to practice a piano lesson and not going to the movies. On the other hand, when the boy has practiced he has the joy of playing well, and when he has failed to practice he has the frustration of being unable to play well. In everyday language it is common to refer to such joy or frustration as a reward or punishment. But if we do so, we need to see that such rewards and punishments are radically different from the first examples. These "rewards and punishments" are intrinsically related to practicing; they have not been arbitrarily imposed from the outside. They flow naturally from the nature of the actions involved.

If we examine the dictionary meanings of reward and punishment, it appears that the extrinsic meanings are the basic meanings of the terms. When these terms are used to describe the joys or frustrations that are inherent in actions, the terms are being used analogically. Because there is only an analogical relationship between the two uses of the terms, it is important to see where the analogy holds and where it breaks down. The analogy between intrinsic rewards and punishments holds insofar as desirable or undesirable consequences result for the person doing or failing to do the action. But if we try to take the analogy much farther, it breaks down. For example, when we are speaking of extrinsic reward or punishment it is natural to ask who is going to give the reward or administer the punishment. There is no answer to such a question when we are dealing with the intrinsic results of an action.

Extrinsic rewards and punishments can serve to motivate a considerable amount of behavior. Most of the penalties attached to the laws of a government are extrinsic in nature. There is no inherent relationship between committing a particular crime and paying a fine or going to prison. If we say that such penalties should not be arbitrary, or that the punishment should fit the crime, we do not mean that the inherent penalty alone should operate. We mean that the amount of punishment inflicted should not go beyond what is called for by the seriousness of the crime. The economic system operates by extrinsic rewards to a considerable extent. There is no inherent relationship between the performing of certain acts of work and the receiving of a paycheck. Most parents use a variety of extrinsic rewards or penalties to keep their children in line.

But there are very definite limits to the motivating power

of extrinsic rewards or punishments. Even in societies where the extrinsic penalties for crimes are severe, crimes are still committed. Sometimes the criminal hopes that he will escape the extrinsic punishment. Inasmuch as the reward or penalty is not inherent in the action involved, there always is a real possibility that the reward or punishment will not follow the action. This lessens the deterrent effects of punishment and the motivating powers of reward. Others, however, commit crimes, even though they may not have great hope of escaping punishment, because the criminal act holds for them satisfactions that exceed their distaste for the penalties. Most highways provide good evidence that the satisfaction of speeding exceeds for many the discomforts of penalties that are placed upon violators of speed laws. Similarly, while the economic system can go quite a way on extrinsic rewards, ultimately there is a point where the lack of intrinsic joy in doing a worthwhile job cannot be compensated for by a paycheck. An important theme in the so-called counter-culture of recent years has been a revolt against working simply for the sake of getting economic rewards. Members of the counterculture have sought those activities which have inherent rewards rather than those which offer only the extrinsic rewards of salaries and wages. And of course, if parents have only extrinsic rewards and penalties to control the behavior of their children, the results are tragic. Unless the parents have established a relationship that gives the children an intrinsic joy in pleasing the parent, extrinsic rewards and punishments will lead to rebellion and bitterness.

The greatest weakness of extrinsic rewards and penalties appears when we deal with compulsive behavior such as we discussed in an earlier chapter. The compulsive eater or drinker cannot be bribed into breaking his or her habits, and threats about the consequences of the compulsion are equally powerless to break the vicious circle. Only when addicts are filled with revulsion against their condition itself is there hope that the bondage will be broken. Inasmuch as we have argued for an analogy between compulsive behavior and the sinful state of being curved in upon oneself, it is not surprising to see that neither state yields to threats and promises.

So far we have been speaking of the law in terms of punishments and rewards in the extrinsic sense of the terms. Hell is commonly pictured as a place of fire and brimstone where the damned suffer eternally. This has no intrinsic relationship to the sins committed; its relationship to sin is as arbitrary as any of the examples we have used above of extrinsic punishments. Similarly, heaven, seen as a realm where the saved can live a life of luxurious ease, is not intrinsically related in any way to righteous living. If we substitute more temporal rewards and punishments for these eschatological pictures, the situation is not changed. The church often has offered a vision of extrinsic rewards and punishments as the motivation for right living. This is the essence of what it means to live under the law.

Does the Scripture teach a system of extrinsic rewards and punishments? There is some evidence that it does in places. For example, Peter on one occasion pointed out to Jesus that the disciples had forsaken all things in order that they might follow him. Jesus answered: "Truly, I say to you, there is no one who has left house or brothers or sisters or mother or father or children or lands, for my sake and for the gospel, who will not receive a hundredfold now in this time, houses, and brothers and sisters and mothers and children and lands, with persecutions, and in the age to come eternal life" (Mark 10:29–30). At first sight, this sounds like an extrinsic reward held before the disciples—a hundredfold return on their investment. However, it would appear that the statement is no more to be taken literally than Jesus' reference several verses earlier about a camel going through the eye of a needle. If Jesus was literally promising a hundred houses to each disciple, the promise was not kept, since the disciples did not cash in on such a reward. Here, as in other places, Jesus seems to be using the language of extrinsic reward to picture the reality of intrinsic satisfaction. Disciples who have given up their homes are at home with God; they belong to the fellowship of the church, which provides them with a "home" wherever they go.

Jesus' paradoxical statement that he who would save his life will lose it, while he who loses his life for Christ's sake will find it (Matt. 16:25) rules out any concept of extrinsic rewards and punishments. What he is saying is that if you have given up house or lands in order to gain a hundred more houses and lands, you will have lost everything. But if you have given of yourself without seeking extrinsic reward, you will have found an intrinsic reward, you will have found true life.

It is my thesis that where Scripture speaks the language of reward and punishment, it usually is using the analogous meaning of the terms to refer to intrinsic results. The Christian is not to hope for a voluptuous heaven of golden streets that is offered to him as an extrinsic reward for a good life on earth. Heaven is a life of loving relationships that a person lives with God and neighbor. The Christian has a hope that this life of relationships will continue beyond death, but the life after death is not an extrinsic reward; it is the continuation of the relationship itself, which is its own reward, and nothing extrinsic could add to it.

Similarly, the Christian is to see punishment as the

separation from God and neighbor in which the sinner lives. At one point Luther argues that sin "is itself the punishment of God." [70] The punishment of sin is an intrinsic element of the sinful situation itself. In the last analysis the sinner is punishing himself by his life lived in separation from God. Hell is not a place where an extrinsic punishment of fire and brimstone is heaped upon the sinner, but it is a life so curved in upon itself that it cannot know the joy that comes from loving God and neighbor.

But even if it be conceded that the rewards and punishments involved are intrinsic to the relationship or lack of relationship with God and neighbor, does that change things? Are we not back again with an appeal to the self-interest of self-centered humanity? Do we not still have the problem that any talk of reward or punishment will motivate self-centered humans to perform good works to win the reward or escape the punishment? Before jumping to this conclusion, we must recall that there is a basic difference between performing a deed for an intrinsic reward and performing a deed for an extrinsic one. It is the difference between playing a game of golf for the sheer joy of playing, and working at a distasteful task in order to get the salary for it. If a person sees Christianity in terms of works-righteousness, he is seeking an extrinsic reward for being a Christian. This means that, hearing Jesus speaking of feeding the poor, he will assume that he must feed the poor so that he can get the reward offered for so doing. But if he approaches Christianity in the spirit of intrinsic values, he will see that being able to help someone in need is its own reward, and that to feed the hungry with one eye on a reward for doing so would be to destroy the whole relationship.

What is being said here forces an examination of how the analogy between using reward and punishment for intrinsic results breaks down when compared to the use of these terms for extrinsic results. If we overlook the way in which the analogy breaks down, we can logically say: The person who feeds the hungry in order to get the reward of heaven and the person who feeds the hungry because feeding the hungry is its own reward are both motivated by the hope of reward. Therefore, there is no difference between them. This reminds us of the old conundrum raised in classes on ethics where we are told that one man, seeing a blind beggar, puts a dollar in his cup because it gives him pleasure to do so. Another man, seeing the same beggar, sneaks a dollar out of his cup because that gives him pleasure. Both men have acted selfishly to seek their own pleasure and, therefore, there is no ethical difference between their actions. This illustration disturbs people because they are certain that there is a basic ethical difference between the two persons. The problem arises because the term "selfishly" is being applied to anyone who gets satisfaction from his action. So defined, the only acts that would be unselfish are those which would be totally unmotivated or purely unconscious. But this is not a normal meaning of "selfish." In ordinary usage we would say that the essence of unselfish behavior is that satisfaction is found in doing a service for another rather than doing something for ourselves.

In the case of feeding the hungry for the reward of heaven or doing it because it is rewarding in itself, there is a confusion similar to that of the two men and the blind beggar. In this case "reward" has only an analogous meaning in the two cases. If we overlook the analogy and assume that reward means the same thing in both cases, we shall see no difference between the two acts. The difference, however, can be put in this way. A self-centered person can be motivated to feed the hungry by any variety of extrinsic rewards. But in doing so he remains self-centered in his actions, since he is still acting to achieve his own ends. But a self-centered person cannot feed the hungry for intrinsic rewards, because the minute his reward is found in the joy of helping others, he has ceased to be self-centered.

People in general do make an ethical distinction between actions performed for intrinsic or extrinsic reasons. When two persons enter into sexual relationships because one or both are seeking an extrinsic reward, we call it prostitution. This presupposes the ideal that sexual relations should be entered into with both parties seeking the intrinsic joy that comes to two persons who are expressing the depth of their relationship to each other. When the reason for one or both entering the relationship is an extrinsic reward, such as monetary payment, it prostitutes the very nature of sex. By analogy the term "prostitution" is used to describe other situations in which an extrinsic reward has become the motivation for action that ought to be done for intrinsic reasons. When an artist creates works because they will bring him profit and not because they are an expression of his art, we say that he has prostituted his talent.

At the time of the Reformation the Reformers again and again were charged with being opposed to good works. The medieval church pictured itself as the defender of good works, while Luther and Calvin were portrayed as being indifferent to the good life. The Reformers vigorously denied this charge. They insisted that their purpose was not to disparage good works, but to see them in the proper perspective. It is not the doing of good works that makes a person righteous, they insisted; rather, it is the righteous person who will perform good works. They made much use of Jesus' point that we can know people by their fruits because "every sound tree bears good fruit, but the bad tree bears evil fruit" (Matt. 7:17). Their point presupposed the distinction between intrinsic and extrinsic motivations for action. The righteous are those who find the reason for doing good works in the joy of doing good works. The unrighteous, however, perform good works only when an extrinsic reward is to be gained or an extrinsic punishment is to be avoided so that their motivation prostitutes the good actions that they perform. Good works performed from self-seeking motives cannot make the performer into a righteous person.

The First Use of the Law Reconsidered

When the distinction between intrinsic and extrinsic rewards for actions is seen, the first use of the law appears in new terms. All too often Protestant churches have used the law to make an extrinsic appeal to potential converts. Heaven is pictured as an extrinsic reward, and hell is an extrinsic torment inflicted upon people. In a less eschatological way, a life of happiness, success, popularity, health, and peace of mind is offered as the extrinsic reward for being Christian. This is contrasted with the life of frustration, meaninglessness, and unhappiness that is the fate of unbelievers. The point of the appeal is that the rewards are always pictured in terms of what the self-centered person naturally wants, and the punishments are those which the self-centered would naturally avoid. The irony in such an approach is that potential converts are promised that, if they will but become Christian, they will receive everything that their sinful hearts desire.

If we begin from the intrinsic implications of actions, preaching the law takes on a new connotation. The law is now preached in terms of holding up the ideal of righteousness. The life of love is portrayed as the selfless concern with God and with fellow human beings. As the picture of love takes form, we find that it comes in judgment over our lives. We recognize that we do not act from love of God and neighbor but from a variety of self-centered motivations. Worse, we recognize that we are in bondage. We are not free to live this life of love, but we are curved in upon ourselves, with the result that even when we try to perform good deeds they are prostituted for the sake of our own extrinsic motivations. Here the law does not serve to fill us with fright in the face of coming punishments or with greed in the face of coming rewards; rather it fills us with a deep discontent with what we are. We come to understand the heartbreaking cry of Paul: "Wretched man that I am! Who will deliver me from this body of death?" (Rom. 7:24).

When the law comes with an extrinsic threat or promise, it stirs the hearer to ask what he must do. This can result in very fervent action, but it leaves a person basically the same person he was before. But when the law comes with an intrinsic appeal, it stirs the hearer to be concerned not first with doing but with being. How, he asks, can I be delivered from what I am; how can I become a new person? Precisely because the extrinsic appeal presupposes what the hearts of the self-centered already desire, it cannot motivate them to desire to be new persons. At best it can only inspire them to do different things to get what they want. But when the intrinsic appeal comes it forces people to see a way of life that they cannot live unless first they become new persons. Jesus was not content to tell people to do different things; he called upon them to be reborn (John 3:3). Repentance in the New Testament is not seen as merely feeling sorry for one's sin; it is seen as a radical turning around, a change in the direction of one's life. When the law is preached as an intrinsic appeal it thus creates the desire to *be* different from what one is.

But there is no power in the law to make us into new

persons. We can no more make ourselves new persons than Nicodemus could reenter his mother's womb and be born again (John 3:4). It is at this point that we recognize most deeply our bondage. Yes, there are many actions that we can perform by an act of willpower, but one thing we cannot do by our willpower is to make ourselves find joy in the doing of those actions that we do not want to do.

Jesus brings this out in a vivid parable of a marriage feast (Matt. 22:1–14). The Kingdom of Heaven, says Jesus, is like a king who gave a marriage feast for his son. When the invited guests failed to come, the king sent out his servants to round up all whom they could find, "both bad and good," so that the wedding hall would be filled. All of this emphasizes God's grace as a love that goes out to seek the lost. As the king was not content to have an empty banquet hall, God is not content to let his children drift from him. But when the wedding guests were gathered, there was one who had no wedding garment. The king became angry and cast him out of the wedding feast. Sometimes modern readers assume that this man had failed to rent a tuxedo for the occasion and, since he was called in from the streets, they wonder if it was not unjust of the king to throw out a man who perhaps could not afford a wedding garment. But according to the customs of the time, a wedding garment was not necessarily an expensive outfit. It could be the everyday clothes of the guest, but when he went to a wedding, he would clean his clothes and decorate them with ribbons or flowers so that his dress would express joy. Jesus' point is that this man was at the wedding, but he was unable to enjoy it. He was there because he was afraid to say "no" to the invitation of the king, but he was not entering into the spirit of the celebration. Jesus is saying that unjoyful obedience to God is disobedience.

If what God requires of me is to give of my money to feed

the hungry, then, by effort of my will, I can do so. But if what God requires of me is that I should love the hungry so that I give of myself joyfully, then I am indeed helpless. No effort of my will can make me enjoy what I do not naturally enjoy doing.

When we look at God's law from the point of view of intrinsic satisfactions we see that our problem is not that we have committed this or that sin. At worst, such sins are only symptoms of a deeper sickness of our very being. Our real problem is never what we have done or failed to do, it is what we are. And it is when we come to see this that suddenly the gospel becomes for us good news. The gospel tells us that even as we are—curved in upon ourselves, shut up in our self-centered interests, God loves us and accepts us. It tells us that while we were yet sinners, Christ died for us. As we begin to experience God's forgiving love we find that, to some degree, our bondage begins to fall away and we are freed to love because first we have been loved. Insofar as God's love becomes a reality for us, we begin to find that there is an inherent joy in the doing of God's will. John tells us that perfect love casts out fear (I John 4:18). The point is that where God's love becomes real we no longer do things because we are afraid that if we do not do them we shall lose God's favors or be cast into some horrible punishment. We do them because we want to do them.

Karl Barth had a profound insight into the meaning of justification when he noted that, seen in the light of grace, God's command is never just another "ought" or duty placed upon us, but rather it is a promise that tells us "You shall be." [71] So seen, says Barth, God's claim is revealed as different from all other claims upon us. All other claims and commands bind us, but God's command sets us free. The other claims "all express to man the suspicion that it might be dangerous to free him, that he would certainly misuse his liberty, that once liberated, he would only create trouble for himself and others." [72] But insofar as a person is drawn into God's forgiving love he is freed to do as he pleases. He is free, precisely because what he most wants to do is the will of God. This is what Augustine saw when he said, "Love, and do what you will."

This enables us to understand a theme that appears in Luther. He says that to experience a sense of ought is already to have fallen into sin. At first it is difficult to understand Luther's point, because it is generally taken for granted that the good person is one whose conscience reminds him of what he ought to do. Our discussion in this chapter helps us to see what Luther had in mind. To experience a sense of ought or duty usually implies that there is within us some reluctance to do what is involved. We do not normally speak of ought or duty where we are engaged in doing what we most want to do. If a young man has to tell himself that he ought to kiss his girl friend good night, then he had better get another girl friend. Luther saw that our relationship to God should be such that we would no more have to feel a sense of "ought" with regard to God's will than a young couple in love feel that they ought to kiss each other. But Luther was aware that the justified person is also a sinner. Thus the Christian does have an experience of ought in his relationship with God. We find again and again that we are reluctant to do God's will, and we have to remind ourselves of what we ought to do. When that occurs we are being reminded that we have fallen into sin because our true relationship with God has been broken. God's command has become for us law instead of gospel, and we need to turn again to the message of the gospel so that the true relationship with God may be restored.

This is how the first use of the law operates to bring us to

Christ. It does not scare us with extrinsic threats or lure us with extrinsic promises. But it does give a vision of true righteousness in a form that forces us to confess that we cannot achieve it by our own efforts. In this confession we admit that we are in bondage, that we cannot be what we would want to be. Thus we are led to see in the gospel of Christ a relationship in which there is the power to free us. In this way, the law can operate as the custodian that can bring us to Christ and bring us back to Christ when we fall away from him.

As we examine this first use of the law, it brings out a rather paradoxical conclusion. Again and again through history we have been told that theologies which teach some element of salvation by works have an optimistic view of human nature, whereas the doctrine of justification involves a pessimistic view. This is half true. Doctrines of salvation by works do teach that if we ought, then we can. They see sufficient health in human nature so that, by an effort of will, we can keep the law and achieve righteousness. In a Christian context such doctrines usually have taught, as Erasmus taught, that our wills are weak and need God's grace—but that our wills do have sufficient power so that they can call on God's grace for the needed help. Over against this view, doctrines of justification hold that human beings are incapable of making themselves righteous. Even if by an act of will they can perform the deed required by law, they cannot, of their own will, do it for the right reasons. It is by grace alone that we can be saved.

There is, however, another way of looking at the question. There is a sense in which the doctrine of justification takes the more optimistic view of human nature. Most doctrines of salvation by works assume that human nature is such that it is necessary to appeal to people's self-interest if they are to be won to Christian faith. If people are to be

won to righteous living, they must be shown an enticing
carrot before them or they must have the whip from behind
to spur them forward. You cannot expect people to be
religious unless they can be convinced that it is good for
them. When people are converted in this spirit, they
naturally ask, Why did this happen to me? when things do
not go right for them. Having been won to Christianity
because of extrinsic rewards and punishments, people feel
betrayed when God does not protect them from the slings
and arrows of outrageous fortune.

The doctrine of justification is more optimistic. It
believes that people will respond to a preaching of the law
that holds up the intrinsic values of the relationship to God
and service to him. Paul says: "Now if I do what I do not
want, I agree that the law is good. So then it is no longer I
that do it, but sin which dwells within me. . . . I can will
what is right, but I cannot do it. For I do not do the good I
want, but the evil I do not want is what I do." (Rom.
7:16–19.) This reveals a human nature that, at its deepest
levels, is capable of recognizing the nature of true righteousness and being attracted to it. People can appreciate that
the truly good person will do something because the deed is
right and not because it pays to be good. They can see that
if I serve either God or neighbor with one eye on what's in it
for me, it is a prostitution of love to both God and neighbor.
And because there is that in human nature which can
recognize this, people can be brought to recognize the
bondage in which they may will what is right but are
unable, of their own power, to achieve it. The doctrine of
justification is, therefore, optimistic enough to maintain that
the law can serve as a custodian to bring people to see their
need of Christ without appealing to their self-serving
motives.

The teaching of Jesus is remarkable in that it makes no

attempt to adorn the gospel with extrinsic rewards. The gospel relationship with God is portrayed as one of joy and happiness. In numerous parables Jesus likens the Kingdom to a marriage feast or other celebration, the prodigal son returns to a celebration, the widow calls in her friends for rejoicing when she finds her lost coin. Jesus did not call his followers to a long-faced religion of joyless asceticism, but the promised joy came from out of the relationship to God and neighbor itself and not from extrinsic enticements.

Instead of holding up extrinsic enticements to move persons to accept the gospel, Jesus told his hearers that they could not follow him unless they took up their cross (Luke 14:27). When one man enthusiastically indicated his willingness to follow him, Jesus made sure that the man was under no illusions. He pointed out that whereas birds have nests and foxes have holes, the Son of man had no place to lay his head (Luke 9:57–58). This clearly told the would-be follower that there were no extrinsic rewards in discipleship. Instead of offering extrinsic rewards, Jesus promised his followers that they would be reviled and persecuted (Matt. 5:10; Mark 10:30; John 15:20). Jesus' presentation of the gospel without extrinsic enticements led Paul to speak of the "peace of God, which passes all understanding" (Phil. 4:7). It passes understanding because it does not look like peace to the man who is curved in upon himself. Such a man finds peace when things are going well for him and his troubles are removed. This is the kind of peace that humanity has always sought in its religions. But this kind of peace is neither promised nor given to the Christian. Jesus himself died on a cross, and his followers have not been protected from any of the ills that beset humanity. Nonetheless there is peace for the Christian, a peace that is intrinsic to the relationship with God in Christ. Whenever attempts are made to spread Christian faith by use of extrinsic rewards and punishments, it becomes difficult, if not impossible, for the convert to understand such peace. For the Reformers the law served at least two purposes. It is a custodian that brings us to Christ and it serves to maintain general law and order in society. The analysis in this chapter indicates that the law operates differently in these two cases. Failure to see the difference can quickly lead to a perverted use of the law as custodian to bring us to Christ.

In operating to maintain law and order in society, the law makes extensive use of extrinsic rewards and punishments. Although the law enforcement authorities are unmindful of why people obey the laws of the land, so long as they do obey, law enforcement is always easier when most people have some motivation for keeping the laws beyond the legal penalties that are applied to the disobedient. But it is of no concern to law enforcement authorities whether people are obedient because of intrinsic desires to obey the law or because of the extrinsic sanctions.

The law as a custodian to bring us to Christ operates on a different basis. The law that brings us to Christ is the law that calls us to act entirely from intrinsic considerations, to do the good because it is good and not because it pays to be good. There are parallels between the operation of the law in the two cases. In both cases the law stands in judgment over people. In both it finds people unworthy. In neither case is the law the good news of Christ, and in neither case does it have the power to make anyone righteous.

But the difference in the law in the two cases is more important than the similarities. The law in its function of creating social stability is concerned with deeds. Its aim is that people should behave in the required way, and the aim is fulfilled even when the only reason that people do behave is that they are afraid not to do so. The law as a custodian to bring us to Christ is concerned with being rather than behaving. It brings us to see not simply that we have done what is wrong, but that what we are is unworthy.

When the church fails to see the distinction between the way the law operates in the two cases, it is tempted to turn its evangelism into a self-seeking appeal. In so doing, it becomes more concerned with what people do than with what they are. This in turn tempts the church to work for laws from the government that will enforce that way of life which ought to be the fruit of the gospel.

The law serves as a custodian to bring us to Christ by holding before us a way of life that is intrinsically desirable but that we are unable to achieve by our own efforts. This helps us to understand another set of Jesus' teachings. In Matt. 5:16 Jesus says, "Let your light so shine before men, that they may see your good works and give glory to your Father who is in heaven." On the other hand, in Matt. 6:1–4 Jesus says: "Beware of practicing your piety before men in order to be seen by them; for then you will have no reward from your Father who is in heaven. Thus, when you give alms, sound no trumpet before you, as the hypocrites do in the synagogues and in the streets, that they may be praised by men. Truly I say to you, they have their reward. But when you give alms, do not let your left hand know what your right hand is doing, so that your alms may be in secret; and your Father who sees in secret will reward you." These passages seem to be in direct contradiction to each other, since the first calls upon Christians to let their good works shine before men, while the second calls them to be so secret in their good works that even their left hand will not know what their right hand is doing. A closer look shows that the passages really complement each other in an important way.

In the second of these passages, Jesus is warning against

the attempt to win favor and honor among men by ostentatious acts of charity. The "hypocrites" who "sound trumpets" so that their good deeds will win attention are seeking extrinsic rewards of fame and honor. The hypocrites are contrasted with the person who does his good deeds secretly and is satisfied with the intrinsic reward of knowing that he is acting in harmony with the will of his heavenly Father. In the first passage, however, Jesus calls upon his followers to let their works shine before men in order to give glory to God. But what actions will give glory to God rather than drawing attention to ourselves? They will be precisely those acts of loving concern for others which are performed with no self-seeking attempt to win some extrinsic reward.

When Christians have debated the place of the law in bringing unbelievers to Christ, they have tended to think of the law as a set of ideals to be preached. Some have felt that the ideals should be preached with threats of extrinsic punishments or promises of extrinsic rewards, while others have argued that the law should be so preached as to move people to see the quality of a relationship with God in which the law is practiced purely for its intrinsic value. To both groups the law has appeared as something to be preached. Without denying that there is a time and a place for the preaching of the law, such preaching is less effective than has been hoped. Abstract ideals, whether based on extrinsic or intrinsic rewards, have a limited ability to motivate people to either action or faith. But when the ideals become incarnate in the life of a person, they take on a new power of attraction. Insofar as the law fills us with a desire for the quality of life that is found in Christ, the law is most likely to operate where we meet that life in the actions of a believer.

Christians often debate among themselves as to what is

the primary task of the Christian. Some argue that the
Christian's first task is to spread the gospel, win converts,
and to be an evangelist. Others argue that the Christian's
first task is to perform acts of love for the neighbor. The
debate is ironical in view of Jesus' words about letting our
light shine before men. Acts of evangelism and acts of love
do not stand in contrast to each other. Acts of love may be
a most effective means of evangelism. When an unbeliever
sees a truly selfless concern for others in the life of a
Christian he may well be led to seek the source of the power
displayed by such a life. On the other hand, of course, if a
Christian displays no love in his life, it is rather futile for
him to preach about the love of God in Christ.

In saying this, there is a real danger. If Christians set out
to do good works for the purpose of winning converts, they
will fail. At best, the results will be the proverbial "rice
Christians," i.e., people who pretend to have Christian faith
so that Christians will continue to do the good works for
them. At worst, people are alienated by the manipulation
that they see implied by the good deeds that are intended to
convert them. When the United States tried to feed the
hungry of the world to prevent them from going communist,
the result was "Yankee Go Home!" signs. Christians will
fare no better if they do good for the sake of converting the
recipients of aid.

The works that lead people to glorify God are the
expressions of love and concern that are given where
needed without any strings attached. Christians cannot,
therefore, set out into the world looking for good deeds to
perform so that God may be glorified. Stephen Leacock
began one of his short stories by describing a certain man as
one who lived his life for others. A fact, observed Leacock,
that you could tell by the harried look in the eyes of the
others. This wry comment points up the fallacy of the

person who goes around looking for good deeds to perform.

In Jesus' parable the good Samaritan was not looking for good deeds to perform (Luke 10:29–37). He was going about his business traveling from Jerusalem to Jericho when he came across a man in dire need. The good Samaritan acted spontaneously to meet the needs of the wounded traveler. He gave selflessly of himself and his possessions and then went on his way without trying to gain honor for himself or the conversion of the traveler. That is the model Jesus holds before us. In such a spirit the spirit of Christ is embodied, and some will be moved by it to seek Christ himself.

VIII

Justification and the Practice of the Church

THROUGHOUT THIS BOOK our thesis has been that the practice of the church has spoken more loudly than its words, and hence that the doctrine of justification has not been communicated in a convincing way. We have attempted to examine the meaning of justification in the light of the teachings of Jesus and the Protestant Reformers. It is necessary to conclude by saying something more about what kind of church practice would be in keeping with the doctrine of justification. Unfortunately, it is always easier to see where something is wrong than it is to say what would be right. It is easier to see where the practice of the church is contrary to its teachings of justification than it is to put forth a program that would be in harmony with the teachings. Furthermore, congregations and individuals face unique problems and situations, so a book cannot lay down universal rules. Therefore I do not make any ambitious claims for what this chapter can achieve. I can only point in a few directions with the hope that others will be stimulated to explore ways of bringing their church's practice into harmony with its teachings.

This study has examined the nature of the righteousness to which God calls us. Jesus said to his disciples, "For I tell you, unless your righteousness exceeds that of the scribes

and Pharisees, you will never enter the kingdom of heaven"
(Matt. 5:20). Christians always try to remove the sting from
these words by supposing that the scribes and Pharisees
were villainous hypocrites. Thus a Christian living a
relatively decent life can feel that he is in a position to thank
God that he is not like the Pharisees. But it is not that
simple. A close look at the Pharisees, either in the New
Testament or in other histories of the times, reveals that
they were models of rectitude and pious behavior. They
were ardent in their obedience to the Jewish law, they were
rigorous in fasting and in tithing of their income, they were
constant and faithful in prayer, and they observed the
Sabbath Day with scrupulous care. But their religion was
by no means limited to the ritual observances. Jesus made
some sharp criticisms of scribes and Pharisees, but he never
hints that they could be found guilty of breaking the letter
of the moral law. In calling us to a righteousness which
exceeds that of the scribes and Pharisees, Jesus was laying a
truly momentous task before us.

Furthermore, it is clear that Jesus is not simply asking for
a more rigorous obedience to the rules. The Pharisees gave
one tenth of all their income to God. In calling for a
righteousness that exceeds that of the Pharisees, Jesus is not
saying that his followers ought to give 15 or 20 percent. On
the contrary, such extension of giving might simply result in
exaggerating the problem that Jesus found in the Pharisees.
The higher righteousness to which Jesus calls his followers
goes beyond the outward practice to the inner state of the
heart and its motivation. It calls for a love of God and
neighbor that results in free and joyful service.

But it is totally impossible for us to make ourselves into
joyfully loving people. We are in bondage to our own
interests, we are curved in upon ourselves. Faced with the
demand for this higher righteousness, we can only confess

that we are sinful and unclean. We are the kind of persons who do those things which cause us to hate what we do (Rom. 7:15). But what we cannot do for ourselves, God has done for us in Christ. Through Jesus we are given the portrayal of God's love, which has come into the far country to seek the wayward prodigals. Even when we were sinners, God loved us and gave himself for us. Because we have first been loved, we find that we are able to love. No doubt our love is still fitful and spasmodic. As Luther continually emphasized, we are at one and the same time justified and sinful; we do not become perfect in this life. But where God's forgiving love has become real for us we cannot be quite the same again. We shall seek again and again to return to the father. We repent, change our ways, and try again. We see the world and our neighbor with new eyes. If this is the essence of justification, what does it say for the practice of the church?

Luther's Paradox

When Luther was wrestling with the practical implications of his doctrine of justification, he presented a suggestive paradox: "A Christian is a perfectly free lord of all, subject to none. A Christian is a perfectly dutiful servant of all, subject to all." [73] Although these statements seem to contradict each other, Luther was convinced that neither one of them was true unless seen in the light of the other. If we were simply to say that the Christian is perfectly free, it would identify Christianity with an anarchistic attitude of "Do your own thing." This could well leave one with a cheap kind of grace that would allow us to live without discipleship to Christ while comforting ourselves that our sins are forgiven. On the other hand, if we said only that a Christian is a perfectly dutiful servant of all, Christianity would be another law. Caught in the toils of our duty, we would have to live a life of service. When taken together, these statements show what the church ought to be.

When Luther speaks of the Christian as being free, he is thinking first of all of freedom from the law. The law comes to us with commandments that restrict what we are to do. It comes armed with extrinsic threats or promises in order that self-interest will bind us to our duty. But the Christian has been freed from the law. He is not under obligation to earn his way into God's presence or to make himself righteous in the eyes of God or man.

Closely combined with freedom from the law is freedom from fear. The extrinsic motivations that come with the law are most often directed at our fears. This is not surprising, because fear is omnipresent in life. We fear sickness, death, the loss of fortune, and so on. But one of the most persistent fears is that of public disapproval. True individuals are difficult to find. Even those nonconformist groups that break radically from the wider society in terms of dress, behavior, and such things as length of hair, tend to conform in their nonconformity. Over against the dominant society the member of such a group appears to be nonconformist, but within the group each member looks and acts similar to every other member of the group. Even in this seeming nonconformity there may be a deeper bondage than that more obvious bondage of the masses. In this way our fears bind us to the demands of the law of our time and place.

In I John 4:18 we are told that perfect love casts out fear. What is pointed to is an intensity of relationship with God that provides a depth of security. As Luther puts it, "If the knowledge of sin or the fear of death should break in upon it, it is ready to hope in the Lord. It does not grow afraid when it hears tidings of evil." [74] Insofar as Christians are certain of God's good will, they do not need to fear the

demands of public opinion. Because they know that
nothing can separate them from the love of God, the fears of
life recede into the background (Rom. 8:38–39). This is not
a security that comes from supposing that evils cannot
happen. The Christian remembers the cross of Christ and
knows that Christians have no fortress to keep them from
the sufferings and defeats of life. But the Christian has
security in the faith that the underlying meaning of life is
beyond ultimate defeat. Behind all fears of specific threats
there lies the basic fear that life itself is meaningless. The
relationship with God gives the Christian the confidence
that life's meaning is assured.

However, if on the one hand the Christian is free, on the
other hand the Christian is the dutiful servant of all.
Justification by grace through faith results in a desire to do
that which is pleasing to God. What pleases God is that we
should have concern for those whom God loves. Again
Luther sums it up for us. "Here faith is truly active through
love (Gal. 5:6), that is, it finds expression in works of the
freest service, cheerfully and lovingly done, with which a
man willingly serves another without hope of reward; and
for himself he is satisfied with the fullness and wealth of his
faith." [75] Freed from the law and fear, a person is able to
express concern for the neighbor without one eye upon his
own interests, and the other eye upon another's approval.
Already rich in his relationship with God, the Christian does
not have to use his neighbor to enrich himself further. The
Christian thus "lives in Christ through faith, in his neighbor
through love." [76]

Luther's Paradox and Church Practice

What does this mean for the practice of the church? It
means that the church should not lay upon its members a

further law. All too often, as has been noted throughout this work, the church puts upon its members (and even more upon its clergy) a set of rules and regulations that must be obeyed if one is to keep in good standing in ecclesiastical circles. Likewise it means that the church will not instill fears in its members in order to make them conform to a required ecclesiastical pattern.

Congregations often make it a rule that their members must attend a certain minimum number of worship services in order to remain in good standing. In a variety of ways the Protestant laity is made to see regular attendance at worship as a duty to be performed. Sermons berate members for nonattendance, various appeals are made to nonattenders to shame them into becoming regular worshipers. The rationalizations that Protestants make for not attending worship services are good evidence that they have been made to feel guilty for staying away. Quite frequently the minister who most loudly berates his members for not attending worship is one who sees no reason why he should attempt to make his services more appealing or meaningful. He is satisfied to depend upon the law to fill the pews and the offering plate.

Despite the pressures to attend worship, there is considerable evidence that Protestantism today faces a crisis in its worship services. For a number of years public opinion polls have indicated that there is a decline in the number of those who regularly attend worship. Many who are firm in their commitment to Christian faith indicate that attending worship services is, at best, a boring chore. Recently I heard a committed layman shock a group of ministers by telling them that he was a Christian, not because of the weekly worship service, but in spite of it. My observations lead me to believe that he spoke for a growing number of church members. It is not unusual to meet people who have ceased to attend worship regularly without in any way feeling that they have given up their Christian faith. Can these trends be reversed by Protestant churches intensifying the discipline and law imposed upon their members?

The doctrine of justification puts more emphasis upon serving the neighbor than upon religious actions such as attending worship services. However, it is important to see the part that is played in the Christian life by the worship service. Where there is the intimate relationship between a person and God that is implied in the doctrine of justification, there will naturally be a desire to worship God. Furthermore, as emphasized earlier, justification does not bring us into a lonely one-to-one relationship with God; it binds us into the fellowship of believers. It is natural for the justified to desire to join with their fellow believers to worship God and to share their faith. Finally, we have seen that the justified person naturally desires to do the will of God. However, Christians know that they are both justified and sinful, they remain fitful, weak, and often impotent in their attempts to do the will of God. They need continually to seek out new strength and power from God's grace. Over the centuries the worship service, centered in the Word and the Sacraments, has proven in the experience of Christians to be a means of grace whereby believers have found new strength for the living of the Christian life.

Through two thousand years of history the Christian church has developed an amazingly diverse number of ways of conducting worship services. From highly structured liturgies to freely spontaneous expressions of the faith, Christian worship has found differing ways to relate believers to God and his Word. But no continuing body of Christians has found that it could dispense with all structures of worship and remain a vital force in the world.

Modern Protestantism, therefore, dares not to be complacent about the present crisis in its worship.

Worship services cannot be restored to health by an exercise of the law. In the light of justification it becomes clear that in no act of the Christian is free and willing performance more important than in worship. Justification brings us into an interpersonal relationship with God; and in all interpersonal relations, actions that are performed out of duty lose their significance. If I give a present to my friend because I feel obligated to do so, it is just a social formality and not an expression of friendship. Similarly, if I attend a worship service out of a sense of duty and obligation, I cannot worship God, I can only go through the motions. Worship, by its very nature, must be a free expression of a loving heart that is gladly given.

A church that patterns its actions after justification will not pursue its members and harangue them into attending worship services. Rather it will present worship as an opportunity for all, a privilege and not a duty. When members fail to attend it will not jump to the conclusion that the fault lies with the nonattenders. It will first ask itself if it has communicated to such persons the joy of the relationship with God. Also it will continually ask if its worship services are patterned so that they encourage the free response of Christians to God. All too often a church operates on the theory that it is the duty of every Christian to be at its worship services, and therefore little attention is paid to the task of making the worship experience more meaningful, joyous, and relevant to the Christian's life.

A few years ago Pierre Berton wrote a highly popular critique of the church, in which he argued that the chief reason for not attending worship services was that they were dull and boring. He said: "Has the Church forgotten that Christianity, in its original vision, is in no sense a doleful religion? With its inherent promise it resembles a marriage far more than a funeral." [77] In the years since Berton wrote this, there have been many attempts by the Protestant churches to put new life into their worship services. A host of experimental liturgies have been tried and discarded. We have learned that just because a liturgy is new and different, it is not necessarily better. Perhaps we are coming to see that the form of a worship service is not as important as the spirit in which it is celebrated. But the fact remains that a church which is committed to justification will continually search for ways to make the worship experience meaningful, joyous, and relevant to the Christian's life. If we fail to do this, we will be falling back into the attitude which assumes that it is the duty of every Christian to attend the worship service, no matter how boring it may be.

If the first implication of Christian freedom is that the church should be free from rules and regulations, the next implication is that the church should provide an environment where fear of being oneself is removed. Christians may sing with fervor "Just as I am," but all too often people are afraid to be themselves in church circles. Instead they find that they are put under great pressure to wear a false mask, to pretend to a righteousness that they do not have. In some church circles, at least, it may win a badge of approval to confess to past sins. Christians can take considerable pleasure in hearing of the depths from which a person has been delivered. But Christians are not nearly so likely to be open to confession of sins of weaknesses that plague a church member in the present.

A number of church members who have joined Alcoholics Anonymous or weight-control groups have reported on the radical difference in the atmosphere that they have found in these groups from the atmosphere found in average congregations. In such groups, organized around a confessed need of the participants, there can be complete honesty. People can tell where they are, they can bare their problems, their failures, their doubts, and their fears. They can do it because they have a confidence that they are in sympathetic company. They are not going to be cast out for failures, they are not going to be scorned or laughed at. They can experience the therapeutic effects of telling all without losing their acceptance. Since there is mutual sharing, there can be mutual help. This is precisely the attitude one would expect in a church that really believed in justification. Our Protestant churches all unite in one way or another every Sunday in confessing: "We are sinful and unclean, we have come short of thy glory." In this way the church acknowledges that it is a community of those who confess they are sinners. But seldom does the atmosphere of the church encourage or even allow its members to spell out the confession in meaningful detail. Having ritually confessed to our sin, we must henceforth put on the false front of righteous piety.

The basis for honesty in one of the groups mentioned above is easy to see. People become members of such a group only when they have recognized that they have a problem that they cannot handle by themselves. They reach out for help and find that they are joined to others in the same condition. The result is a fellowship of mutual help in which honesty comes naturally. Having joined the group, one has confessed the worst. Later confessions can only spell out the details. Furthermore, the confession is made to those who have also confessed to the same problem, so no one is in a position to cast the first stone. The members may admonish and exhort each other even as they cheer each other's victories, but never do they rule a stumbling member out, beyond the pale. So long as a person is still seeking help he is welcomed with love and sympathy. After all, how could the members ostracize such a person when each one knows that he or she is likewise only one drink away from the gutter or one dessert away from a return to obesity?

Should we not expect the same attitudes in a church that believes in justification by grace alone through faith alone? By joining the church we confess that we are sinners. A few years ago a book on the church appeared with the appropriate title, *For Sinners Only*. To become a member of the church is to confess not only that we are sinners but that we cannot handle our problems by ourselves. We are reaching out for help from beyond ourselves. Looking to God's grace, we are joined in the church to others in the same condition. Should we not expect that within the fellowship of the church the confessed sinners would be able to confess honestly to the particular forms of their sin? Should we not expect that, since all our fellow members are also confessed sinners, there will be no one in a position to cast the first stone? Why then is it that so often the church fails to provide an atmosphere in which people do feel free to be themselves?

One of the problems is that the church is conscious of being the protector of the public morality. In a variety of ways it has been at pains to present itself to the world as having a particular concern with the good life and with being prepared to hunt down "sin" wherever it appears. As a result of this, when a person joins the church the culture at large does not see it as a confession of sin, but rather as a claim to be on the side of righteousness. Because society thinks of joining the church as a claim to having achieved righteousness, there is great joy when a church member shows an Achilles' heel. Sin within the church always seems much worse than sin outside the church. In the eyes of society, church members who stumble are seen as having compounded their sin by adding hypocrisy to it. They have pretended to a righteousness that they do not possess. Because this social attitude is well known to church members, they become extremely sensitive about their public image. If the church is to witness to the world, it feels that it must become beyond reproach in its behavior. When, therefore, some member falls from the straight and narrow way, it is seen as bringing disgrace upon the whole membership and undermining its witness to the world. In such an atmosphere there is great pressure upon each member to keep up a front of complete rectitude and untiring piety. This is why confession of sins of the past is highly commendable but confession of sin in the present is discouraged. Ironically enough, in this concern for its witness, the church ends in a total failure to witness to its central theme that God accepts us as we are.

Training in the view that the church is the collection of the morally superior begins at an early age. When the child enters the church building he or she is expected to act with unnatural decorum. A few years ago a father was sitting in front of me in church with his seven- or eight-year old son. As we reached the Kyrie in the liturgy the boy turned around to stare at me. Just as we were singing "Lord, have mercy" the father grabbed hold of the boy's ear and viciously tugged his head around to face front. The scene was an excellent parable. The words being sung were in perfect harmony with the doctrine of justification. But were not the words and their message drowned out for that boy, perhaps forever, by the action of the father? The action loudly proclaimed that life in the church must be free from the normal actions and weaknesses of daily life.

Alcoholics Anonymous or weight-control groups are not so heavily burdened with a sense of duty to uphold public

morality. Therefore they can be singled-minded in their
concern to give help to the helpless. In the process they do
make their contribution to public morality and public
health. A church that lived in the spirit of the doctrine of
justification would make a contribution to public morality.
But the contribution would be a by-product, its central
purpose would be to communicate God's love and help to
the helpless. It would be far more concerned to deal with
human beings where they are than with trying to be an
example of virtue. Then it would become as easy to be
oneself without pretense in the church as it is in these other
groups.

There is another dimension to this problem of acceptance
of each other within the church. In the foregoing I have
been assuming that it was a case of confessing that which
would be considered sinful by both those who confessed
and by those to whom they confessed. The situation,
however, becomes more complicated when there is disagreement as to the sinfulness of the actions involved. On a
great many issues that face the Christian in the modern
world there is no clear Biblical teaching to give direction for
action. Even where there is Biblical teaching, there is often
a serious problem of how we should apply in our situation
the words that were spoken to a radically different situation.
For example, we have already noted that Jesus' words about
divorce were spoken in a social context where a man had
the right to divorce his wife with or without good cause and
where, when divorced, she had no further claim upon him
for support. On the other hand, the wife could not divorce
the husband, no matter how grave the provocation. How
should we apply Jesus' words to the totally different
situation in the modern world where both parties have a
right to seek divorce and where the husband normally has to
pay alimony to the divorced wife? Only the most literalistic

of legalists could claim that divorce is divorce, and that what Jesus said about divorce applies without qualification to the modern situation. Where the Bible is silent or does not speak clearly to modern circumstances, equally sincere Christians will come to different conclusions about what a Christian ought to do.

There is a further reason why Christians who are equally committed to pleasing God will not always agree upon what will please God. The doctrine of justification means that Christian life is not guided by a set of rules and regulations. The Christian is called to act in a spirit of love to God and neighbor. But Christians will not always agree upon which actions are most loving in concrete situations. I have argued that there is no "agapeic calculus" which enables us to work out precisely which actions will maximize love in any given situation. As a result, Christians will inevitably come to different conclusions as to what they should do.

The differences of Christians are painfully evident in the life of the church. Christians find themselves disagreeing with fellow Christians about war and pacifism and, as the Vietnam war made evident, even when Christians may agree on war in general, they may be divided upon whether or not a particular war is a just war. Christians disagree with Christians on programs of political action, divorce, birth control, abortion, smoking, drinking alcoholic beverages, the use of various drugs, dancing, gambling, hunting for pleasure, and a host of other issues. There is always some pain involved when a fellow Christian blithely goes about doing something which others feel to be out of keeping with faith in Christ. It becomes particularly painful when what one believes to be a vital issue is considered by another Christian to be a trivial matter.

What happens when Christians differ on which actions are implied by Christian faith? All too often it results in a

breaking of fellowship between them. Sometimes there is a
rule of the denomination or congregation which officially
excommunicates or disciplines a person who violates the
majority opinion. Thus some denominations have stead-
fastly refused to remarry divorced persons or ordain those
who would not take an oath pledging themselves not to
smoke or drink alcoholic beverages. But most frequently
the fellowship is broken in unofficial ways. Some will
withhold donations from a congregation or denomination
that has taken ethical stands with which a person disagrees.
In some cases the donations are withheld simply because
the church involved has allowed some of its members to act
in ways that others disapprove. Sometimes in subtle ways,
and often in not so subtle ways, one group of Christians lets
another one know that they have put themselves beyond the
pale because they have done things which the first group
considered sinful. When different denominations are discussing church union, it is not at all unusual to find that
ethical issues are a greater barrier to union than theology.
Concerned Christians ask how they can be united with a
church that allows the drinking of alcohol, ordains women,
or takes a stand for racial equality.

This tendency of Christians to reject fellow Christians
because of different ethical conclusions often results in a
lack of openness and honesty between Christians. Knowing
that our fellow Christian disapproves strongly of some
action which we find in harmony with Christ, we are careful
not to perform the act in his presence or to let him learn of
our doing it. When Christians get together they carefully
avoid bringing up political or social issues because they fear
that disagreement in these areas will destroy their Christian
fellowship.

When differing Christian ethical convictions are involved,
it has become common to appeal to the concept of the

"weaker brother." This is rooted in Biblical passages such as I Cor., chs. 8 and 9, or Rom. 14:15 to 15:1. In these passages Paul argues that, although certain things—such as eating meat that has been offered to pagan gods—are lawful to the Christian, a Christian ought to act in love. If his eating becomes "a stumbling block to the weak" (I Cor. 8:9), the Christian should let love for the weaker brother override the exercise of his Christian freedom. If we examine these passages closely, we find that Paul has in mind actions of Christians that might result in some other person falling from faith in Christ. Thus he speaks of actions by which "this weak man is destroyed, the brother for whom Christ died" (I Cor. 8:11). Likewise he can say, "Do not let what you eat cause the ruin of one for whom Christ died" (Rom. 14:15). As such, Paul's teaching is important for the Christian life. The doctrine of justification leads us to love the neighbor, and thus we cannot hold our freedom more precious than our neighbor's relationship to Christ. Important as Christian freedom is, surely all would agree that it must be foregone when its exercise would destroy the faith of another person.

But in church life things are not this simple. The people who claim to be offended by another's actions are not likely to think of themselves as "weaker brothers." On the contrary, they think of themselves as so strong in the faith that they know that the other's action is unworthy of a Christian. If the person who is attacked is to remain in fellowship with them and maintain the peace of the church, then he or she must accede to the critic's demands. In such a case, Paul's passages on the weaker brother are not as relevant as his passages on circumcision. When some of the Jewish Christians demanded that all Gentile converts to Christianity be circumcised and that they obey the Jewish law, Paul forcefully attacked them. When one group of

Christians today insists that all Christians must perform certain acts (or refrain from certain acts), it becomes a blurring of the nature of justification by grace through faith. Such demands must be resisted, not only in the name of Christian liberty, but as a witness to justification itself.

Of course, the situation is usually even more complicated. When the appeal is made to concern for the weaker brother, it is always a good question as to who is the weaker brother. Some Christians see the weaker brethren as those who will be repelled by a Christianity that seems to be dedicated to the keeping of rules and regulations. In such cases it may appear that the most effective witness to the weaker brother is a firm resistance to the demands of fellow Christians who would impose their convictions upon all Christians.

What does the doctrine of justification say to these problems? The person who has experienced justification will seek to do that which is pleasing to God and thus will seek the will of God in all things. However, when the justified person attempts to do this it soon becomes apparent that, in many cases, there are no clear-cut directions for action. A choice must be made as responsibly as possible. So long as we are aware that we are justified by grace alone through faith alone, we know that our relationship to God does not depend upon what we do and neither does it depend upon our correctness in making the right choice about what is the proper action to perform.

When we find that fellow Christians have chosen differently from ourselves, it should cause concern. It is important that we enter into dialogue with them. We must listen to their reasons for their decision, and we have the right to expect that they will listen to ours. Perhaps one of us will be persuaded and change his opinions. But very frequently this does not occur. The history of Christianity gives little reason for being optimistic that Christians will be able to achieve complete agreement upon all ethical decisions. What then should be our reaction?

If I believe that I am justified by grace through faith, then I am keenly aware that my sins are forgiven. I stand where I stand before God, not because of my good deeds or my brilliant ethical decisions, but because God loves and forgives me. Therefore, even though it seems to me that a fellow Christian is acting in a way that is seriously out of harmony with Jesus Christ, dare I cast the first stone? Dare I say that I am right in this matter and he is wrong? How could I decide in these circumstances that his differing convictions are sufficient reason for me to cut off fellowship with him and to cast him into the outer darkness? Certainly I shall continue to try to persuade him of his "errors." And, if I am to do that, I must be open to listen to his attempts to persuade me.

A church that patterned its practice in the light of justification would be one in which there was a free acceptance of the members by each other. Agreement upon ethical conduct would not be a prerequisite to fellowship. In such a church each Christian would feel free to practice and defend his choices without fear that he would be cast beyond the pale for so doing. Freedom from fear would thus include the freedom from fearing that we would lose our place in the community of the church because of our honest convictions about the nature of the Christian life.

A Church That Is Free to Lose Its Life

An important element in the freedom from fear that we should expect from churches is freedom from obsessive fear about the survival of the institution. Jesus said: "For whoever would save his life will lose it, and whoever loses his life for my sake will find it" (Matt. 16:25). This is a theme that the church, as an institution, ought to take seriously. During the 1960's there was considerable brave talk about the church being willing to lose its life, and there were even some actions that seemed to be predicated upon this willingness. But since we have entered what Martin Marty has called "the securitism of the seventies" we do not hear much about this anymore.

We need always to recall what Emil Brunner emphasized: the church is not an institution; it is a fellowship of people based upon their fellowship with Christ.[78] A people will always *have* institutions, but a people is not an institution. The institution of the church is simply an instrument that the people of God use in their mission and work. Because the institution is an instrument, an ultimate concern to preserve the institution is not a mark of faith but of idolatry.

When the church, as an institution, has an idolatrous fear of losing its life, it tends to preserve itself through appeals that fall short of the gospel. In an earlier chapter we quoted Luther to the effect that it would be better for all churches to close than to remain open by appealing to selfish interests. Luther pictured a church that was ready to lose its life in order to find it. But this is not a spirit that the church displays too often. When the stewardship campaign gets under way in most congregations, it is a time when justification by grace alone through faith alone is suspended for the duration. Congregations have property that must be maintained and salaries to be paid. They are expected to have some concern for helping the needy. Thus, to survive, congregations have to get money, and the simplest way to get money is to appeal to self-centered interests. Protestant stewardship campaigns are not as crude as the money-raising campaigns of Tetzel in the time of the Reformation, who promised that the soul of some loved one would flee from purgatory when the money clinked in the box. But they do have sophisticated ways of persuading people that giving is good for them. How frightened churches get when someone suggests that donations to churches should lose their income-tax-exempt status. Without the sugarcoating of tax exemptions it is feared that the bottom would drop out of church giving. In subtle ways the members are promised that they will get close to God if they but give to the church. When all else fails, recalcitrant members are nagged, harangued, embarrassed, and shamed into increasing their pledges.

In our first chapter we noted that a recent study of the attitudes of Protestants revealed a confusion in the area of giving. On the one hand, strong support was expressed for the works-righteousness answer that financial giving brings us close to God. On the other hand, a high proportion of the same people declared that the basic reason for giving to the church was gratitude to God. The reason for this confusion is no doubt the nature of stewardship campaigns. Being good Protestants, dedicated to the doctrine of justification, we keep telling people that the primary reason to give ought to be gratitude to God. But then, just to make sure that the money comes in, we add the appeals to self-interest. It is not surprising, therefore, that the same study finds that the actual practice of giving by Protestants does not correspond to the sound theological reasons that they enunciate.[79]

A church that believed in justification and was freed from its fear for the preservation of the institution would develop its stewardship so that it enhanced the credibility of the doctrine of justification. Such a church would believe not only that God loves a cheerful giver (II Cor. 9:7) but also that God desires no other kind of giver. Therefore, it would make no effort to beg, cajole, or entice the recalcitrant to give to the church. It would preach, teach, and practice the good news of God's love in season and out of season. When the time came for a stewardship emphasis it would consist solely in educating the membership in what the church could and would do if it had sufficient funds. Those who were filled with the love of God would cheerfully give for those activities that seemed to serve God. If such an approach did not bring sufficient funds to keep the institution of the church going, then it could well be concluded that the institution was so near failing in its purpose for existence that it could without loss be allowed to die. That seems exactly what Luther had in mind when he said that it would be better to let the church die than to resort to fear to get people to support it.

Freedom from an idolatrous concern to preserve the institution of the church ought to help in bringing the missionary outreach of the church into harmony with the doctrine of justification. Christianity is a missionary religion because it believes in a missionary God. Central to the doctrine of justification is the view of God as one who came to seek and to save the lost. If the church is to witness to the God who was not content to sit in heaven and wait for people to come to him, then the church must be prepared to go out to share the good news that it has received. However, an ardent desire to win converts is not necessarily an expression of authentic faith. The Pharisees were noted for their missionary zeal, but Jesus said to them, "Woe to you, scribes and Pharisees, hypocrites! for you traverse sea and land to make a single proselyte and when he becomes a proselyte, you make him twice as much a child of hell as yourselves" (Matt. 23:15).

Many things may pervert the church's attempt to spread the gospel. However, in the light of justification, it is clear that a major problem will always arise when the attempt to win converts has a self-seeking motive. Inasmuch as the church is called to tell of God's selfless love for his wayward children, the message loses credibility to the degree that the messenger reveals self-seeking motives. Where a church has fear for its survival as an institution, it is always tempted to seek converts to save its own life.

The self-seeking of the church may appear in a very crass form. It is well known that a large mortgage on a church's property can effectively fill its membership with a desire to travel sea and land to find converts. But the self-seeking of the church may not be so crude. It is natural to our sinful selves that we long to remake others in our own image. All too often the attempt to win people to the faith is a thin disguise for an attempt to remake them so that they will be like ourselves. Therefore, we are not simply desirous of keeping the institution of the church in existence; we are also determined to keep its life and practice in harmony with our own attitudes and practices. And thus our evangelism seeks converts who will preserve the *status quo* of the congregation. In terms of race, ethnic background, and economic status, as well as in terms of belief and practice, we want to preserve our congregation in its present patterns. Only when we have been freed from fear for the preservation of the institution will we dare to present the gospel and allow its spirit to blow where it wills and bear its own fruits in the hearers.

There is one saying of Jesus about spreading the gospel that often sounds strange. When sending out his disciples to tell the good news, Jesus said, "And if any one will not receive you or listen to your words, shake off the dust from your feet as you leave that house or town" (Matt. 10:14). At first reading this sounds very unlike the Jesus who told us that God is like a shepherd seeking out a lost sheep or like a poor woman frantically sweeping her floor to find a lost coin. Contrary to such teaching, here he seems to be telling his disciples to give up rather quickly on a potential convert. To shake off the dust sounds like a rather calloused way of leaving persons to their fate.

But when we look at these words in the light of the doctrine of justification they take on different meaning. Justification seeks the righteousness that flows from a willing heart. God does not drag us kicking and screaming into his Kingdom. He wins us by love or not at all. Therefore, what Jesus is saying here is that the missionary must be prepared to let the potential convert make a free choice. All too often we have seen people harangued and harassed by those who would convert them. In a college setting, I have seen a person selected as a potential convert and have observed how the zealous missionaries then divide up the day and night so that there is always one or more of the missionaries with the person, working to win a decision. The result is a rather distasteful form of brainwashing. To such enthusiasts Jesus is saying: If certain persons do not hear you gladly, quit bugging them, shake off the dust from your feet and take your word to where it will be received gladly.

At the heart of the doctrine of justification is a respect for the person. God loves his children too much to violate their personhood in order to win them to himself. Because the goal of justification is a freely persuaded person, evangelism that fails to respect the selfhood of the other person will inevitably falsify the meaning of justification. However, where there is an anxious concern with the institution's welfare there is likely to be an evangelism that will be prepared to use any form of psychological pressure in order to get the prospect into the fold.

The Servanthood of the Church

The theme of freedom from fear about the preservation of the institution of the church provides a good point to turn to the second aspect of Luther's paradox. If, on the one hand the Christian is a free lord of all, on the other hand he is a servant of all. A church that is freed from concern for its own preservation is one that is freed to serve God in his world.

Luther believed that the Christian would be a servant because the experience of justification binds him to his neighbor with bonds of love. Luther put it vividly: "I will therefore give myself as a Christ to my neighbor, just as Christ offered himself to me." [80] To a hidebound brand of orthodoxy these are dangerous words, for if we encourage Christians to think of being Christs to their neighbors, will that not undermine the Christian doctrine of the uniqueness and divinity of Christ? Even many loyal Lutherans have felt that Luther went too far in saying this; yet Luther seems solidly Biblical at this point. In the New Testament the church is referred to as "the body of Christ" (e.g., I Cor. 12:12–31; Eph. 3:6; 4:12). Does this not mean that the people who belong to the church are to embody Christ in their world and thus, in a real sense, to be Christs for their neighbors? As Jesus incarnated God's love in his earthly life, so the church is to incarnate Christ's love in its action. Christ said that he did not come to be ministered to but to minister and to give his life as a ransom for many (Mark 10:45). The church, therefore, as Christ's body, will be more concerned to serve than it is to preserve itself.

The call of the church to be the servant of all, even as Jesus made himself the servant of all, is a natural outcome of the experience of justification. Drawn out of themselves by God's love for them, Christians respond by loving God and those whom God loves—their neighbors. This loving service becomes a part of proclaiming the gospel. If the church sits comfortably behind its walls, it may still preach of God seeking the lost, but its action will speak against its words. The church is called to embody Christ's concern to go where the people are to tell the good news. If the church passes by on the other side of human need, it will cast doubt upon even the most brilliant preaching and teaching about the love of God. If the church is a judgmental institution, continually damning the weaknesses of human beings, how difficult it will be to persuade people that God forgives sins. If the church is primarily concerned to preserve its institutions, how believable will it be when it says that God so loved the world that he gave his son (John 3:16)?

For several years the *Yearbook of American and Canadian Churches,* which reports on church statistics, has shown that about 80 percent of the money received by churches is spent within the local congregations. This leaves only 20 percent for the wider work of the church. But even here a large amount goes to support the institutions of the church, denominational hierarchy, seminaries, and the like. No doubt some of the 80 percent kept in the local congregations is used for purposes other than maintaining the institution. But even on the most generous of suppositions, a major proportion of a dollar given to most churches goes to preserve ecclesiastical institutions. Churches seriously need to ask what their budgets are saying about the doctrine of justification which the churches are preaching.

When we speak about the church being a servant of others it raises in the modern world the old debate about whether the church should simply seek "to save souls" or whether its gospel has social and political implications. This would have seemed a strange debate to the Reformers.

Although they began with the need to bring the good news of God's salvation to individuals, Luther and Calvin had no doubts about the social and political thrust of the gospel. In fact, for the Reformers, their rediscovery of the doctrine of justification inevitably resulted in their recognition of the importance of the sociopolitical sphere as an area in which we are called to serve God.

For Luther the logic that led from justification to social involvement went like this. Works-righteousness involved the doing of religious works of piety to please God. When we come to see that our justification is by grace through faith, however, we see that God is not pleased by such activities. We please God by expressing love to those whom God loves. In a typical passage Luther attacks the medieval church because of its understanding of good works. "If you ask . . . whether they consider it a good work when a man works at his trade, walks, stands, eats, drinks, sleeps, and does all kinds of works for the nourishment of his body or for the common welfare, and whether they believe that God is well pleased with them, you will find that they say no, and that they define good works so narrowly that they are made to consist only of praying in church, fasting, and almsgiving." [81] To believe in justification, however, is to see that what pleases God is precisely the daily work in the calling of a person whereby he contributes to the well-being of his society and thus of his neighbor. But the welfare of society, and of our neighbors, depends upon good civil government.

In an earlier chapter we saw that Luther taught that there are two kingdoms or governments. There is the church, where the Word of God operates through persuasion, and there is the civil government, where the sword is used to maintain peace, harmony, and justice. Insofar as a Christian does freely and joyfully the will of God, he does not need the sword of the state to make him obey. But, as

Luther says wryly, "Christians are few and far between." [82]
For the mass of humanity the state is necessary, and this
holds true for Christians too, since, and insofar as, all
Christians remain imperfect and sinful. Because the state is
necessary to the welfare of humanity and since the justified
Christian will attempt to please God by serving the
humanity that God loves, the Christian will be politically
active. Luther sums it up by saying: "Just as he performs all
other works of love which he himself does not need—he
does not visit the sick in order that he himself may be made
well, or feed others because he himself needs food—so he
serves the governing authority not because he needs it but
for the sake of others, that they may be protected and that
the wicked may not become worse. . . . If he did not so
serve he would be acting not as a Christian but even
contrary to love; he would also be setting a bad example to
others." [83]

Luther spoke out of the late medieval situation, in which
the governments were essentially autocratic. At that time
most Christians could contribute little to politics except to
obey the rulers. Most of Luther's political comments,
therefore, were directed to the rulers. To understand their
significance for today we need to translate Luther's views
into the new situation that has developed where power has
democratically spread to a wider group of citizens.

If we look at Luther from the standpoint of twentieth-
century Christians in a democratic society, it is evident that
Luther could not imagine a presentation of Christianity that
did not call all Christians to social and political activity. For
example, noting that Paul speaks of the governing authority
as a servant of God, Luther affirms that Christians must not
allow it to be exercised only by the heathen. On the
contrary: "What can be the meaning of the phrase, 'It is
God's servant,' except that governing authority is by its very

nature such that through it one may serve God? Now it would be quite un-Christian to say that there is any service of God in which a Christian should not or must not take part, when service of God is actually more characteristic of Christians than of anyone else." [84] This calls contemporary Christians, with their political rights and privileges, to serve God in the political sphere.

Because Luther emphasized the two-kingdom theory and separated the work of church and state, many Lutherans have assumed that the only task of the church is to preach the gospel and attempt to win individuals while the problems of government are left to others. This completely misses Luther's point in dividing the two kingdoms. They are divided because their methods of working are quite different but God's will and plan for humanity requires both. Therefore, each Christian is called to serve God in both kingdoms. Luther would no doubt have opposed using the church as a pressure group to win political battles, but he firmly believed that the church should so teach and lead Christians that they would see the need for, and the nature of, Christian service in the political realm. Luther would have branded as heresy that kind of Christianity which has ignored the social implications of the gospel. If the church does not lead its members to see the social and political implications of Christian faith, people will be led to see service to God as being identical with service to the institution of the church, and thus we are well on our way back to a view of salvation by works.

When we turn to Calvin we see that he was as much concerned as Luther that the Christian should recognize the social and political implications of his faith. Calvin affirmed that civil government "is equally as necessary to mankind as bread and water, light and air, and far more excellent." [85] Furthermore, Calvin insisted that the political rulers, whom

he referred to as "magistrates," were called upon to act for
God. "Wherefore no doubt ought now to be entertained by
any person that civil magistracy is a calling not only holy
and legitimate, but far the most sacred and honourable in
human life." [86] Again as we translate Calvin's words into
the situation of the twentieth century where Christians are
citizens of a democratic nation, it is evident that Calvin
would see the need for Christians to be engaged in social
and political action.

It is a strange irony that in recent years Protestant
churches have had so much difficulty in balancing a ministry
to individuals with a ministry to tackle social and political
problems. Some churches have been carried away with the
ideals of a social gospel and seem to have nothing to say to
individuals. Other churches have set themselves the goal of
"winning souls for Christ" and have rigorously excluded any
social or political implications from their preaching or
ministry. This is ironical because the rediscovery of the
centrality of the doctrine of justification by the Reformers
led them to see clearly that God calls us to both aspects of
ministry.

Where the doctrine of justification is taken seriously, the
church cannot overlook its mandate to declare the good
news of God's forgiving love to all persons. But the justified
person is in a relationship where he seeks to do God's will,
and this calls him to love the neighbor. At no time in
history could a full love to the neighbor be expressed
without taking into account the social and political sphere.
We do not live like Robinson Crusoes on desert islands; we
live in societies, and the way in which society is governed
has a great deal to do with everyone's welfare. Therefore,
as Luther and Calvin saw, good government plays an
important role in loving our neighbors. But in the modern
technological age, this is even more the case than ever

before. In a world faced with food shortages, energy crises, and limits to growth, it is not enough for individuals to feed and clothe the hungry individuals they may meet. We need to organize all the resources of political power to see that there is justice for all and to protect the weak from the powerful. Where millions suffer because of their race, it is not enough for Christians to express love to individuals that they meet who are of another race; we must work for laws that protect minority groups from the racism that destroys life and dignity.

Although Luther and Calvin saw clearly that the doctrine of justification calls us to political concern, their positions were still clouded by the medieval attitudes in which they were raised. Both men put a great emphasis upon obedience to the governing authorities, even when those authorities were evil. Calvin could say that "it is impossible to resist the magistrate without, at the same time, resisting God himself." [87] He then went on to point out that this remains true even if the magistrate himself fails to perform his duties properly.[88] Luther was equally concerned that Christians should obey the state. When the peasants of Germany were demanding justice, Luther wrote a tract in which he found much merit in their demands and said, "We have no one on earth to thank for this disastrous rebellion, except you princes and lords, and especially you blind bishops and mad priests and monks, whose hearts are hardened, even to the present day." [89] However, despite recognizing the justice of the peasants' cause, when they persisted in their revolt Luther wrote another tract that has become the darkest mark against his name. In it he called upon the ruling class to put down the rebellion without mercy. "Let whoever can stab, smite, slay. If you die in doing it, good for you! A more blessed death can never be yours." [90] In Luther's eyes the sins of the rulers against the peasants paled into insignificance beside the action of the peasants in revolting against the lawful rulers.

Not only were Luther and Calvin under the influence of medieval society, which extolled obedience to superiors, they were also frightened by what they themselves had done. In overthrowing the prestige of the medieval church they had undermined one of the basic foundations of order in their world. Quite obviously they feared that their action might have a "domino effect." With the authority of the church under question, would not all ruling powers likewise fall? Did they not stand on the verge of anarchy? Both men seem to have had an almost neurotic fear of anarchy which led them to overemphasize Scripture passages such as Rom. 13:1–7, or I Peter 2:13–17. Both men admitted that if it became a question of serving God or man, we would have to serve God, but both seemed to be reluctant to see that choice anywhere except where it involved the most important elements of theological doctrine.

The life and teaching of Jesus hardly supports the Reformers' views of obedience to rulers. Jesus spoke contemptuously of his king, calling him a "fox" (Luke 13:32). Standing before Pilate, Jesus refused to answer some questions, and he reminded Pilate that all of his power came from above and that therefore Pilate was not a final authority (John 19:10–11). In cleansing the Temple, Jesus openly broke the civil laws and defied the ruling powers in Jerusalem. Inasmuch as the Jewish authorities had no power to execute a person, Jesus was put to death by the Roman government. This would indicate that the rulers saw in Jesus something more than a religious heretic. When the crowd told Pilate that he would be no friend of Caesar's if he let Jesus go, it says rather plainly that there was reason for believing that Jesus was not a friend of Caesar (John 19:12).

If we examine the question of governmental authority in the light of the doctrine of justification, we shall not be as ready as Luther and Calvin to prohibit all disobedience to rulers. Luther and Calvin saw quite rightly that civil government is necessary because of the sin of humanity. Because most people will not do the right and good thing joyfully and of their own free will, there is the need for the power of the state to enforce peace, order, and justice. But, precisely because all are sinful, we must assume that rulers are also sinful. Therefore, as Reinhold Niebuhr saw so clearly, governments are never simply a protection against injustice, they are also strongholds of injustice. Although the Christian ought to seek to have the government protect the weak from the strong, in fact most governments tend to protect the strong from the weak. The sword is wielded to maintain the *status quo* and all its inequities. Therefore, we should be prepared to see that service to God rather than to man may sometimes bring us into conflict with the rulers over many more matters than just the niceties of theological doctrine or ecclesiastical practice. We must affirm that there are times and places where obedience to God can only mean disobedience and resistance to the rulers.

The Church and Its Social Obligations

Luther and Calvin agreed upon the necessity for Christians to be involved in the social and political world. But there were some differences in their emphases upon the relationships of church and state.

As we have seen in other contexts, Luther was convinced that the state should not legislate in the realm of Christian faith. Against heretics, the only sword that should be used is the sword of God's word. To those who would argue that the government was not forcing men to believe but that it was just seeing that no one should be deceived by false doctrine, Luther answers that this is a task for the bishops to handle. And he goes on to say, "Heresy is a spiritual matter which you cannot hack to pieces with iron, consume with fire, or drown in water." [91] Furthermore, notes Luther, faith and heresy are never so strong as when they are opposed with force. As a result he asks, "What do you gain by strengthening heresy in the heart, while weakening only its outward expression and forcing the tongue to lie?" [92]

Luther also felt that the state ought not to attempt to legislate the kind of behavior that should be the willing fruit of a heart given freely to God in Christ. Luther probably would have been shocked at the idea of legislation requiring attendance at worship services. Even in vital matters such as marriage, Luther did not feel that the church should try to dictate decisions to the state. [93] In short, Luther believed that the Christian who was active in civil government should act to express love for the neighbor by bringing about peace, justice, and the protection of the weak. He should not use the state to promote the gospel.

Luther's teaching, as seen, is simple, clear, and in complete keeping with the doctrine of justification. Unfortunately, later in his life, Luther did make some concessions that compromised his basic position. He suggested that rulers were justified in not allowing blasphemy to be proclaimed in their realm. Then he went on to define blasphemy as a denial of "an article of faith clearly grounded in Scripture and believed throughout the world by all Christendom, such as the articles we teach children in the Creed." [94] This concession sounds particularly dangerous against the background of our pluralistic modern society. However, we have to see it against the background of the homogeneous medieval society, where Christianity was accepted as the official religion. I believe that it would be a serious distortion of Luther's basic position if we should try to justify this concession in today's world.

In Calvin we find a more pronounced tendency to justify the Christian in using the state to promote the gospel. In addition to using the state to express love to the neighbor, Calvin believed that Christians should use it to glorify God. This meant that the state should prevent heresy, promote true doctrine, and enforce general Christian behavior. As Calvin put it, "This civil government is designed, as long as we live in this world, to cherish and support the external worship of God, to preserve the pure doctrine of religion, to defend the constitution of the Church. . . ." [95] Against the view that the rulers should not legislate in spiritual matters, Calvin said that it was folly to suppose that the governors whom God had appointed should only decide secular matters while disregarding "that which is of far greater importance—the pure worship of himself according to the rule of his law." [96] Calvin thus encouraged the state to enforce religious orthodoxy. If the blackest mark against Luther was his letter encouraging the rulers to crush the peasants, the blackest mark against Calvin was his complicity in the burning of Servetus in Geneva for heresy. When later Calvinists succeeded in getting legislation to require attendance at worship services, it would appear to be in keeping with Calvin's teachings.

At this point we must argue that Luther's emphasis on the role of the state was more in harmony with the doctrine of justification than was Calvin's. Inasmuch as justification aims at a righteousness that comes freely from the heart of a person, the state is powerless to enforce such righteousness. Since God seeks a free interpersonal relationship with his children, the state cannot legislate anyone into it. The God who is revealed in justification cannot be honored by legally enforced beliefs or actions. The state is fitted to regulate the relationships between people in society, it can maintain law, order, peace, and further justice, but it cannot aid an individual in becoming personally righteous and it cannot help one to be related more intimately to God.

Earlier we saw that Protestant churches blur their teaching of justification by seeking laws that legislate personal morality. We can now see that this tendency has roots in Calvin's view that the state is called to maintain God's honor and glory, and perhaps in Luther's later concession that the state should prohibit blasphemy. A church that patterns its practice on its doctrine of justification, however, will be one that is prepared to take the gamble that God himself took when he sought to win the free response of his children without the use of external force. As such, it will take seriously the earlier teachings of Luther about the church-state relationship.

Conclusion

This last chapter was necessary, but it is dangerous. It was necessary because it has been my thesis that the practice of the Protestant churches has contradicted what they have preached about justification. Therefore, it was appropriate to make some attempt to describe the kind of practice that would enhance rather than hinder the teaching of justification. It is dangerous, however, because it may give the impression that we have ended on a note of law. It is like the story of the old Lutheran pastor who preached a Reformation Day sermon. Beautifully he portrayed the nature of justification by grace alone through faith alone, but unfortunately he did not end his sermon soon enough. His concluding sentence was, "And so, dear friends, if you will just go to church, read your Bibles, and say your prayers, God will take all of you to his heaven." Since in this final chapter I have tried to see what sorts of action would be appropriate to a church that would put justification into practice, I may end up by leaving the impression that we are saved by our works after all.

Therefore it is necessary to make a few points in conclusion. This chapter has not been written with any idea that the church is required to make itself righteous or pleasing in God's sight. On the contrary, the church, consisting of people who know that they have been accepted, forgiven, and loved by God, is desirous of finding ways to serve God. In particular, the church is concerned that it should not act in a way that would blur for others the good news of the gracious God who accepts us as we are.

In the second place, this chapter is written without forgetting that Christians are always both justified and sinful. We make no claim for perfection. At best we are on the way, and thus we do not pretend that we have arrived. The practice of the church will always fall short of what it preaches, and therefore it will continue to live by forgiveness and not by its achievements or merits. As Christians we have every right to hope that a life lived in God's presence will bear fruit in sanctification. Calvin was particularly strong in emphasizing that there should be progress in our sanctification. He could say of sanctification, "No man will be so unhappy, but that he may every day make some progress, however small." [97] Luther likewise expected that the Christian's life would show some progress in overcoming obvious sins. But Luther did not speak of any continual progress in sanctification because he was aware that as one overcomes the more gross and obvious sins the more subtle sins such as pride become a greater temptation. Thus it is precisely the dedicated and concerned church which is in the greatest danger of falling into a spirit of judgmental self-righteousness that makes the doctrine of justification incredible.

It is important to see why, in the Reformation, it was argued that the true church exists where the gospel is preached and the sacraments are administered in accordance with the Scripture. A few years ago, in his popular book *The Secular City*, Harvey Cox argued that this Reformation definition of the church is no longer satisfactory. The marks of the true church, argued Cox, must include service and fellowship as well as preaching the gospel and administering sacraments.[98] The problem is that if we allow the definition of the true church to include these marks of sanctification, then the church becomes the work of man. If we can only be the true church where we are living in service and providing Christian fellowship, we are again under the law, forced to save ourselves by our works. The Reformers saw clearly that if justification comes by grace alone through faith alone, then the marks of the true church cannot be found by looking at the lives or practice of the membership. The true church exists where the good news of the gracious God is being faithfully proclaimed and where the sacraments are being offered as a means of receiving God's grace. The hope for the church remains always in God and not in the church's membership.

This leads to a third point about this chapter. God is able to speak even through an imperfect church. Our thesis in this book has been that the practice of the church has blurred and made incredible the doctrine of justification. But this does not mean that the doctrine does not speak with power to some despite the practice of the church. Even in a church marred by judgmental self-righteousness, if the good news of justification is being preached, it will come home to some who need to know that they are forgiven and accepted as they are.

Karl Barth once pointed out that we always need to distinguish between what God can do and what God calls us to do. God can, for example, speak through a poorly prepared or heretical sermon. But this does not mean that the ministers of the church are called to preach poorly prepared heresy. It remains an important article of faith for the church that God can speak to people despite all the failures of the church, but this does not mean that we are called to ignore our failures. God has used for his purposes, and will continue to use, a church that fails to live by its teaching of justification. But this is no reason why Christians should not be concerned to bring the practice of the church more closely into harmony with its teaching.

As I have examined the doctrine of justification, I have emphasized that, although we are not saved by the good works that we perform, nonetheless the relationship with God that is offered in justification will bear fruit. Justification will bring about sanctification. If we consider the reformation or renewal of the church in the light of the doctrine of justification, we shall always see it as a free and joyful response to what God has done. We shall never see it as something which we must first do in order that we may become the true church. True renewal of the church itself will always be a fruit of the gospel and never the result of obeying the demands of the law.

NOTES

1. See Theodore G. Tappert (ed. and tr.), *The Book of Concord* (Muhlenberg Press, 1959), p. 292.

2. John Calvin, *Institutes of the Christian Religion*, tr. by John Allen (Presbyterian Board of Christian Education, n.d.), Book III, ch. xi, para. 1. (Hereafter this will be referred to as Calvin, *Institutes*.)

3. Lawrence K. Kersten, *The Lutheran Ethic* (Wayne State University Press, 1970), pp. 92, 156.

4. Merton P. Strommen *et al.*, *A Study of Generations* (Augsburg Publishing House, 1972). See Ch. 6.

5. *Ibid.*, p. 369.

6. *Ibid.*, p. 145.

7. Douglas W. Johnson and George W. Cornell, *Punctured Preconceptions: What North American Christians Think About the Church* (Friendship Press, 1972), p. 52.

8. Reinhold Niebuhr, *The Irony of American History* (Charles Scribner's Sons, 1952), p. 50.

9. *Ibid.*, pp. 50–51.

10. Myer S. Kripke, "Letter to a Kind Lady," *The Christian Century*, Vol. XC, No. 45 (Nov. 28, 1973), p. 1173.

11. Langdon Gilkey, *How the Church Can Minister to the World Without Losing Itself* (Harper & Row, Publishers, Inc., 1964), p. 40.

12. See Martin Luther, "Lectures on Romans," *Glosses and Scholia*, Luther's Works, Vol. 25, p. 286. (Please note that, unless

otherwise indicated, quotations from Luther are from the English translation edited by Jaroslav Pelikan [Vols. 1–30] and Helmut Lehmann [Vols. 31–55], published by Concordia Publishing House and Fortress Press, 1958–.)

13. Ibid., p. 220.
14. Ibid., pp. 294–295.
15. Ibid., p. 381.
16. Ibid., p. 449.
17. Ibid., p. 234.
18. Luther, "Temporal Authority: To What Extent It Should Be Obeyed," The Christian in Society II, Luther's Works, Vol. 45, p. 105.
19. Ibid.
20. Ibid., p. 94.
21. Rosemary Ruether, Liberation Theology (Paulist/Newman Press, 1972), p. 176.
22. See Will Herberg, Protestant—Catholic—Jew (Doubleday & Company, Inc., 1955); Martin Marty, The New Shape of American Religion (Harper & Brothers, 1959); A. Roy Eckardt, The Surge of Piety in America (Association Press, 1958).
23. Reinhold Niebuhr, Beyond Tragedy (Charles Scribner's Sons, 1938), pp. 69–87.
24. Ibid., pp. 82–83.
25. Dietrich Bonhoeffer, Prisoner for God: Letters and Papers from Prison, ed. by Eberhard Bethge, tr. by Reginald H. Fuller (The Macmillan Company, 1954), p. 159.
26. James Cone, A Black Theology of Liberation (J. B. Lippincott Company, 1970), p. 194.
27. Calvin, Institutes III. ii. 2.
28. See Tappert (ed.), The Book of Concord, p. 432.
29. Luther, Lectures on Galatians, I, Luther's Works, Vol. 26, pp. 305–306.
30. Luther, A Commentary on St. Paul's Epistle to the Galatians, tr. by Philip S. Watson (Fleming H. Revell Company), p. 482.
31. Dietrich Bonhoeffer, The Cost of Discipleship, tr. by R. H. Fuller (SCM Press, Ltd., 1948), p. 35.

32. Ernest Gellner, *Words and Things: A Critical Account of Linguistic Philosophy and a Study in Ideology* (Beacon Press, Inc., 1960), p. 31.

33. Calvin, *Institutes* II. ii. 7.

34. Luther, "The Bondage of the Will," *Career of the Reformer III*, Luther's Works, Vol. 33, p. 68.

35. Luther, "The Freedom of a Christian," *Career of the Reformer I*, Luther's Works, Vol. 31, p. 371.

36. Dietrich Bonhoeffer, *Ethics*, tr. by N. H. Smith (The Macmillan Company, 1955), p. 3.

37. James Cone, *Black Theology and Black Power* (The Seabury Press, Inc., 1969), p. 71.

38. Luther, "Lectures on Romans," Luther's Works, Vol. 25, p. 345.

39. Luther, *Table Talk*, Luther's Works, Vol. 54, p. 127.

40. Calvin, *Institutes* II. vii. 8.

41. *Ibid.*, II. vii. 10.

42. *Ibid.*, II. vii. 12.

43. *Ibid.*

44. See Tappert (ed.), *The Book of Concord*, pp. 303–304.

45. *Ibid.*, p. 480.

46. Gerhard Ebeling, *Luther: An Introduction to His Thought*, tr. by R. A. Wilson (Fortress Press, 1970), p. 133.

47. Luther, "The Freedom of a Christian," Luther's Works, Vol. 31, p. 348.

48. *Ibid.*, p. 368.

49. Luther, "Lectures on Romans," Luther's Works, Vol. 25, p. 60.

50. Calvin, *Institutes* II. vii. 13.

51. *Ibid.*, II. vii. 14.

52. *Ibid.*, II. vii. 15.

53. Tappert (ed.), *The Book of Concord*, pp. 480–481.

54. Luther, "Lectures on Romans," Luther's Works, Vol. 25, p. 244.

55. *Ibid.*, p. 450.

56. *Ibid.*, p. 493.

57. Luther, "The Sermon on the Mount," *Sermon on the Mount and the Magnificat*, Luther's Works, Vol. 21, pp. 3–4.

58. Joseph Fletcher, *Situation Ethics* (The Westminster Press, 1966), p. 95.

59. *Ibid.*, p. 98.

60. Cone, *Black Theology and Black Power*, pp. 35–36.

61. Luther, "Exhortation to All Clergy Assembled at Augsburg, 1530," *Career of the Reformer IV*, Luther's Works, Vol. 34, p. 21.

62. Luther, "The Freedom of a Christian," Luther's Works, Vol. 31, pp. 365–366.

63. Paul Althaus, *The Divine Command: A New Perspective on Law and Gospel*, tr. by Franklin Sherman (Fortress Press, 1966), pp. 3 ff.

64. Luther, *Lectures on Galatians, I*, Luther's Works, Vol. 26, p. 309.

65. Calvin, *Institutes* II. vii. 4.

66. *Ibid.*, II. vii. 7.

67. Bonhoeffer, *Prisoner for God*, p. 146.

68. Calvin, *Institutes* III. ii. 7.

69. Luther, "Lectures on Romans," Luther's Works, Vol. 25, p. 466.

70. *Ibid.*, p. 162.

71. See Karl Barth, "Gospel and Law" in his *Community, State and Church* (The National Student Christian Federation, 1960), p. 87.

72. Karl Barth, *Church Dogmatics*, Vol. II, Part 2, ed. by G. W. Bromiley and T. F. Torrance (T. & T. Clark, 1957), p. 585.

73. Luther, "The Freedom of a Christian," Luther's Works, Vol. 31, p. 344.

74. *Ibid.*, p. 357.

75. *Ibid.*, p. 365.

76. *Ibid.*, p. 371.

77. Pierre Berton, *The Comfortable Pew* (McClelland & Stewart, Ltd., 1965), p. 106.

78. Emil Brunner, *The Christian Doctrine of the Church, Faith,*

and the Consummation, tr. by David Cairns and T. H. L. Parker (The Westminster Press, 1962), pp. 20 ff.

79. Johnson and Cornell, *Punctured Preconceptions,* pp. 144–145.

80. Luther, "The Freedom of a Christian," *Luther's Works,* Vol. 31, p. 367.

81. Luther, "Treatise on Good Works," *The Christian in Society I,* Luther's Works, Vol. 44, p. 24.

82. Luther, "Temporal Authority," Luther's Works, Vol. 45, p. 91.

83. *Ibid.,* p. 94.

84. *Ibid.,* p. 100.

85. Calvin, *Institutes* IV. xx. 3.

86. *Ibid.,* IV. xx. 4.

87. *Ibid.,* IV. xx. 23.

88. *Ibid.,* IV. xx. 24–29.

89. Luther, "Admonition to Peace," *The Christian in Society III,* Luther's Works, Vol. 46, p. 19.

90. Luther, "Against the Robbing and Murdering Hordes of Peasants," Luther's Works, Vol. 46, p. 54.

91. Luther, "Temporal Authority," Luther's Works, Vol. 45, p. 114.

92. *Ibid.,* p. 115.

93. See Luther, *Table Talk,* Luther's Works, Vol. 54, p. 363.

94. Luther, "Psalm 82," *Selected Psalms II,* Luther's Works, Vol. 13, p. 61.

95. Calvin, *Institutes* IV. xx. 2.

96. *Ibid.,* IV. xx. 9.

97. Calvin, *Institutes* III. vi. 5.

98. See Harvey Cox, *The Secular City* (The Macmillan Company, 1965), p. 145.

INDEX